# LIFE
## AMONG THE
# LUTHERANS

# Life among the Lutherans

## Garrison Keillor

EDITED BY HOLLY HARDEN

Augsburg Books

MINNEAPOLIS

LIFE AMONG THE LUTHERANS

Published by Augsburg Books, an imprint of Augsburg Fortress. All rights reserved.
Except for brief quotations in critical articles or reviews, no part of this book may
be reproduced in any manner without prior written permission from the publisher.
Visit http://www.augsburgfortress.org/copyrights/ or write to Permissions, Augsburg
Fortress, Box 1209, Minneapolis, MN 55440.

Cover image: Town Church copyright Joseph Brown, Gallery 344 Ltd
Cover design: Laurie Ingram
Book design: Christy J. P. Barker

*Library of Congress Cataloging-in-Publication Data*

Keillor, Garrison.
Life among the Lutherans / Garrison Keillor.
p. cm.
ISBN 978-0-8066-7061-4 (alk. paper)
1. Lake Wobegon (Minn. : Imaginary place)—Fiction. 2. Lutherans—Minnesota—
Fiction. 3. Minnesota—Social life and customs—Fiction. I. Title.

PS3561.E3755L535 2009
813'.54—dc22

2009008712

The paper used in this publication meets the minimum requirements of American
National Standard for Information Sciences—Permanence of Paper for Printed
Library Materials, ANSI Z329.48-1984.

Manufactured in the U.S.A.

13   12   11   10   09        2   3   4   5   6   7   8   9   10

# Contents

# Introduction

I don't know much about Lutherans, and that is one reason I've told stories about them over the years, so I could learn. I grew up fundamentalist in a small sect, the Sanctified Brethren, who believed in separation from the world and looked on Lutherans as worldly, ignorant of the finer points of Scripture, a jovial band of large people who made too much of Christmas and took much too much pride in their damn choirs, more a social club like the Elks than a gathering of the devout. That haughty attitude was baked into me, and it stuck even though I left the Brethren tent forty years ago. So when I first started telling stories about Lutherans, it was with a faint sneer on my lips.

I was younger then, and as we all know, a sneer is a young man's way of disguising his ignorance. I lived in St. Paul and moved in rarefied circles of pale aesthetes inhaling the fumes of self-regard, and the less said about that the better. But doing *A Prairie Home Companion* on a stage in front of real people was a great education, and it took me to Moorhead, Minnesota, home of Concordia College, and other places where people of a true Wobegonian stripe came to see the show, and that was humbling. It was like the experience of a singer friend of mine who studied opera in Minnesota and California and then took a job singing in Verona: it suddenly dawned on him that he was singing Puccini to people who knew the words. And they would know if he tried to fake it.

As I know now, the Lutherans are a humble and generous and for-giving people, and they have shown this to me again and again. They have shamed me with their generosity. They keep inviting me to speak in their churches. They lavish praise on me—"You must have known my family!" they cry. "You describe us so accurately." That is most assuredly not true.

But Lutherans are merciless in their goodness. I was once given an honorary doctorate at Gustavus Adolphus College and sat on the dais as a man read a citation that made me weep for shame, it was such a bundle of lies, and then I had to stand up and be hooded as people clapped, and then—one last humiliation—I had to give a commencement speech! This is how Lutherans punish a sinner—they put him up front and hang him with compliments. (Just as the congregation of Lake Wobegon Lutheran does when they put out the commemorative volume of Pastor David Ingqvist's best sermons, *To Know Him Is to Love Him*, and he glances at them and realizes they have chosen the worst.) The place for any true Christian, as any Lutheran knows, is in the back of the hall ushering, or else in the basement making coffee and heating up the cinnamon rolls. Virtue lies in humble service. It's the jerks who stand up and give big self-congratulatory speeches.

And I feel like a jerk sometimes, sashaying out onstage and telling the story about the twenty-four Lutheran pastors who were aboard a pontoon boat when it tipped over and hot coals from the barbecue in the stern went skittering across the deck and over the rails into five feet of water, and even as I tell the story, I know that a righteous man would not be doing this. A righteous man would be out in the lobby taking tickets or outdoors parking cars. The righteous man would be serving lunch in the basement. He would be doing good work that is always anonymous and humbling.

What keeps me plugging away is the feeling, which has grown over the years, that I have it in me to become a journalist if I will just pay attention and that there is some truth in, for example, the story of the former wrestler turned preacher. And Ernie and Irma Lundeen and their Performing Gospel Birds. The little crises of organists. The long, inexplicable marriage of Clarence and Arlene Bunsen. The dramas of the pastor's daughter and the vigilance of Val Tollefson on the church board.

There are baptisms and weddings, picnics and funerals, confirmations and the National Church Ushers Competition and deer hunting and snowstorms. And the return of one of those twenty-four pastors who, after the pontoon boat went down, left the ministry. He meets Pastor Ingqvist, who is raking leaves and who has often considered leaving the ministry but remains and every Sunday, in the company of his fellow Lutherans, attempts to lift up his heart and theirs to the Lord.

I've been invited to preach in Lutheran churches, and I have always declined. I once accepted an offer to preach at Grace Cathedral on Nob Hill in San Francisco, and my Sunday happened to be a couple of weeks after September 11, 2001; I did my best, but I have not been tempted to return to the pulpit ever since.

The people who occupy the pews of Lake Wobegon Lutheran on Sunday are ordinary people, doing their best to be good and walk straight in a world that seems to reward the crooked and mock the righteous. They gather together and give alms to the poor; they sing, "Lift every voice and sing till earth and heaven ring," so that tears come to your eyes; and they pray to God, "Create in me a clean heart, O God, and renew a right spirit within me. Cast me not away from thy presence, and take not thy Holy Spirit from me. Restore unto me the joy of thy salvation. . . ." And then they go home and put on their work clothes and tend their flower beds and groom their lawns. While they do their best to love each other, they also watch each other very closely. There is gossip, on occasion. There are cold-shoulder treatments and grudges and ferocious rivalries. Despite one's best efforts, envy of the achievements of someone else's children is a tough thing to deny.

So back to church they go, seeking forgiveness and grace. Church is the place where, like Robert Frost said, when you need to go there, they have to take you in. You can come back every Sunday promptly, or come on Easter and Christmas if that's what you can manage. If you wander in and find a potluck supper going on and you forgot to bring a hotdish, it's okay—Lutherans always have extra. And there always is coffee. It may not be the best coffee, but it's good enough.

*Garrison Keillor*

*Life is complicated, so think small.*

# I

# It Could Be Worse

I am a cheerful man, even in the dark, and it's all thanks to a good Lutheran mother. When I was a boy, if I came around looking glum and mopey, she said, "What's the matter? Did the dog pee on your cinnamon toast?" and the thought of our old black mutt raising his hind leg in the *pas de dog* and peeing on toast made me giggle. I was a beanpole boy, and my hair was the color of wet straw. I loved to read adventure books and ride my bike and shoot baskets in the driveway and tell jokes. My dad, Byron, was a little edgy, expecting the worst, saving glass jars and paper clips, turning off lights and cranking down the thermostat to keep our family out of the poorhouse, but Mother was well composed, a true Lutheran, and taught me to Cheer up, Make yourself useful, Mind your manners, and, above all, Don't feel sorry for yourself. In Minnesota, you learn to avoid self-pity as if it were poison ivy in the woods. Winter is not a personal experience; everyone else is as cold as you are, so don't complain about it too much. Even if your cinnamon toast gets peed on. It could be worse.

Being Lutheran, Mother believed that self-pity is a deadly sin and so is nostalgia, and she had no time for either. She'd sat at the bedside of her beloved sister, Dotty, dying of scarlet fever in the summer of 1934; she held Dotty's hand as the sky turned dark from their father's fields blowing away in the drought; she cleaned Dotty, wiped her, told her stories, changed the sheets; and out of the nightmare summer she emerged stronger, confident that life would be wondrous, or at least bearable.

It was a good place to grow up in, Lake Wobegon. Kids migrated around town as free as birds and did their stuff, put on coronations and executions in the long, dim train shed and the deserted depot, fought the Indian wars, made ice forts and lobbed grenades at each other, dammed up the spring melt in the gutters, swam at the beach, raced bikes in the alley. You were free, but you knew how to behave. You didn't smart off to your elders, and if a lady you didn't know came by and told you to blow your nose, you blew it. Your parents sent you off to school with lunch money and told you to be polite and do what the teacher said, and if there was a problem at school, it was most likely your fault and not the school's. Your parents were large and slow afoot and they did not read books about parenting, and when they gathered with other adults, at Lutheran church suppers or family get-togethers, they didn't talk about schools or about prevailing theories of child development. They did not weave their lives around yours. They had their own lives, which were mysterious to you.

I remember the day I graduated from tricycle to shiny new two-wheeler, a big day. I wobbled down Green Street and made a U-turn and waved to Mother on the front porch, and she wasn't there. She had tired of watching me and gone in. I was shocked at her lack of interest. I went racing around the corner onto McKinley Street, riding *very* fast so I would have big tales to tell her, and I raced down the hill past the Catholic church and the old black mutt ran out to greet me and I swerved and skidded on loose gravel and tumbled off the bike onto the pavement and skinned myself and lay on the tar, weeping, hoping for someone to come pick me up, but nobody came. The dog barked at me to get up. I limped three blocks home with the skin scraped off my forearm and knee, my eyes brimming with tears, and when I came into the kitchen, she looked down at me and said, "It's only a scrape. Go wash it off. You're okay."

And when I had washed, she sat me down with a toasted cheese sandwich and told me the story of Wotan and Frigga. "Wotan, or Odin, was the father of the gods, and his wife, Frigga, was the earth goddess who brought summer, and the god of war, Thor, was the winter god, and the god of peace was Frey. So from Odin we get Wednesday; from Thor, Thursday; from Frey, Friday—Sunday and Monday, of course, refer to the sun and moon—which leaves Saturday and Tuesday. Wotan and Frigga had a boy named Sidney, and Thor had a daughter named Toots. They fell in love, and one day Sidney went to find Toots and steal her away, but Thor sent a big wind and Sidney rode his bicycle too fast and fell and skinned his knee, and that's why Saturday is a day off, so we can think about it and remember not to ride our bikes so fast." She gave me a fresh, soft peanut butter cookie. She wiped the last remaining tears from my cheek. She said, "Go outside and play. You're all right."

In Lake Wobegon, you learned about being All Right. Life is complicated, so think small. You can't live life in raging torrents; you have to take it one day at a time. And if you need drama, read Dickens. My dad said, "You can't plant corn and date women at the same time. It doesn't work." One thing at a time. The lust for world domination does not make for the good life. It's the life of the raccoon, a swashbuckling animal who goes screaming into battle one spring night, races around, wins a mate, carries on a heroic raccoon career, only to be driven from the creek bed the next spring by a young stud who leaves teeth marks in your butt and takes away your girlfriend, and you lie wounded and weeping in the ditch. Later that night, you crawl out of the sumac and hurl yourself into the path of oncoming headlights. Your gruesome carcass lies on the hot asphalt to be picked at by crows. Nobody misses you much. Your babies grow up and do the same thing. Nothing is learned. This is a life for bank robbers. It is not a life for sensible people.

The urge to be top dog is a bad urge. Inevitable tragedy. A sensible person seeks to be at peace, to read books, know the neighbors, take walks, enjoy his portion, live to be eighty, and wind up fat and happy, although a little wistful when the first coronary walks up and slugs him in the chest. Nobody is meant to be a star. Charisma is pure fiction, and so is brilliance. It's the dummies who sit on the dais, and it's the smart people who sit in the dark near the exits. That is the Lake Wobegon view of life.

*The urge to perform is no indication that a person has talent.*
*We know that. And remember: Lutherans, generally speaking,*
*are not the ones up on stage.*

## 2

# The Young Lutheran's Guide to the Orchestra

Lutherans are a calm, stoical, modest people, haunted by guilt, fearful of looking ridiculous, so they feel more secure if they are surrounded by people who are dressed like them and who are doing the same thing they are, and this leads many Lutherans to consider a career in the orchestra. The uniform is nice. Black. You never need to do laundry. The music is so passionate, and that's nice, to be associated with passion without anyone blaming you personally. Of course, you have to put up with someone waving his stick in your face, but you simply ignore him and wait until the others play; that's the Lutheran way. It's a good job, the orchestra. Unfortunately, there is the question of talent.

Many musicians go to the audition and take out their instruments to warm up and then hear the other people warming up and put their instruments back in their cases and go enroll in broadcasting school. The urge to perform is no indication that a person has talent. We know that. And remember: Lutherans, generally speaking, are not the ones up on stage.

Lutherans are the ones who hand you your program as you come in.

Generally, the musicians aren't Lutheran, though some of them take drugs to make them feel Lutheran.

In the Bible we see references to music, but it was played in praise of the Lord, not for amusement. The apostles did not play instruments or attend concerts. The only art form that our Lord embraced was fiction, when he came out with the parables. So if you, a young Lutheran, want to be a musician, if you feel you have real musical talent—not just that you are talented in comparison to the rest of your family—you ought to ask yourself, *Which instrument is the best one for a Lutheran to play? If our Lord had played an instrument, which one might He have chosen?* Assuming He was Lutheran.

Probably not a French horn . . . The French horn is too hard to play. It just is. You mess up on a French horn, there's no hiding it. Playing a bad note on a French horn is like breaking wind at your mother's funeral; it's unthinkable. So of course a horn player sits and thinks about nothing else.

Should you play the bassoon? Not if you have self-esteem issues, you shouldn't. The bassoon is a noble instrument, and like most noble things, it's always on the verge of sounding ridiculous. When you hear a bassoon on a movie soundtrack, you know you're watching a cartoon. About six notes on the bassoon sound great, and the others are on the verge of sounding ridiculous.

Many Lutherans start out playing clarinets in marching band, and it's a good-natured instrument, but you soon find out: the clarinet is a handful of problems. If it's hot, it goes sharp; if it's dry, the reed is no good; if it's humid, the keys stick; and if it's cold, the instrument can crack. A clarinet is always on the verge of collapse.

The oboe is a sensuous instrument. When you hear it on a movie soundtrack, you know you probably should not be watching this with your children. The oboe plays, and it means she's going to take her shirt off and there's going to be heavy breathing.

But the life of an oboist is pure frustration. You have to blow so hard sometimes your back turns purple. You're always making new reeds and they're never quite right and they don't last long. The oboe player is the one who sounds the A when the orchestra tunes up. He works hard to get a perfect 440 A, knowing it doesn't matter—the violins are going to tune sharp anyway.

The English horn is lovely and frustrating and easily gets out of control and honks. It takes a long time to get really good on the English horn, and meanwhile there's less of a market for English hornists than there is for ugly babies. This is discouraging.

The flute is the star of the wind section, the big shot. Jean-Pierre Rampal, James Galway, both millionaires. (How many millionaire bassoonists can you name real fast?) If you can learn how to blow across a tiny hole with your head tilted, it could be a good career move. But the flute is too spiritual for a Lutheran. You start playing one, and the next thing you know, you're wearing a caftan and sitting in a grove of redwoods playing at a healing ceremony conducted by someone named Starflower Moonbright at which people are whanging on drums and affirming each other's personhood and hugging. And Lutherans do not hug. Only for the holidays, only with relatives, and only sideways.

The last member of the woodwind family is the piccolo, a piercing instrument. When it plays a solo passage, every gynecologist in the auditorium gets up and goes to the telephone. Somehow the piccolo doesn't feel comfortable in an orchestra. It's the woodwind that really wants to be a Fender Stratocaster.

We come now to the string section. Sometimes you assume that the string players are smarter because they sit in the front, but is there evidence for this? I don't know. The bass, for example, is a necessary instrument; you can't get along without bass. Music has to have a bottom, just as you do, or it would fall over, but the parts are really rather boring. Sometimes the composer throws in some sixteenth notes and makes them hustle and flap around for a while, but otherwise, a bass player's mind tends to wander.

Mainly what they think about is transportation. Playing a bass is sort of like playing a sofa, in a way. Bass players think, *What if she forgot? How am I going to get this thing home?*

Cellists are such pleasant people. The way they sit with their arms around their instruments, they look like parents at the day care center zipping up little snowsuits.

And cellists love their instruments as if they were children; they love that rich, mellow tone.

Cellists can become so absorbed in their beautiful tone that sometimes when the symphony ends, they look up in surprise. They still have a page left to play.

Violists are good people. They have no ego, because there is so little solo music written for them and so many jokes told about them. When there is a long viola passage, the rest of the orchestra stares at them in astonishment, like watching people who are blind shooting baskets. Violists feel moody about this, and late at night they get together for burritos and red wine from a carton and talk about getting out of music and into telemarketing.

The first violins are proud people. During breaks in rehearsal, they like to sit in their chairs and go over the hard parts, so everyone knows it wasn't them who screwed up.

The first violins hardly ever look at the conductor. They know that he takes his tempo from them anyway, so what's to look at? It's the winds he's conducting—the conducting has nothing to do with them.

The violin is for people who express themselves; it's not for Lutherans. It has soul, it weeps, it cries out, it argues. Honey, face it: this is a Jewish instrument. There is no Itzhak Peterson or Pinchas Soderberg or Jascha Hansen. If you're Jewish, go, play already. Lutherans? I don't think so.

The second violins sit with the percussionists right behind them. It's like having a gun to the back of your head. And you play accompaniment. That's what you do. You're a thoroughbred hitched up to a beer wagon. Somebody has to pull it, and you're the one. The curse of the second violins: any of these people can go home and play the Beethoven Concerto perfectly; they just can't do it if anybody is listening.

Let's be clear on one thing about the brass section. There are times when the rest of the orchestra wishes the brass were playing in another room, and not necessarily in the same building. Composers have written so few notes for brass forte because after they play, your interest in music goes away for a while. The brass include a number of men who used to be in the construction trades and went into music because there's less dust. The tuba player is the only member of the orchestra who bowls over 250 and gets his deer every year and changes his own oil. In his locker downstairs, he keeps a pair of lederhosen for freelance jobs. But there's only one tuba, and he's it—and these guys never die.

The trombonist is an invisible person in the orchestra. Many of the string players didn't know there was one. When they saw him backstage, they assumed he was a stagehand working out a plumbing problem.

The trombonist is almost never allowed to give full voice, except in Wagner or Bruckner. Otherwise, the trombone is basically a thickener, like cornstarch.

The trumpet is an unhealthy instrument; you have to blow so hard that after a big passage, you may be unable to remember your own Social Security number. That's why trumpeters never call other musicians by name; they just say, "Hey, guy," or "Hey, kid."

Trumpet players don't want to wear black; they'd prefer red. They're soloists trapped in an orchestra member's body. They like to play loud, and when they see the players in front of them wince, they know it's loud enough. Most people who have keeled over dead at concerts were stricken during trumpet passages, and most of them were glad to go.

There are two places in the orchestra for a Lutheran, and one is the percussion section. You learn patience in percussion.

Pages and pages of music go by while the percussionist sits and waits, silently counting the bars like a hunter in the blind waiting for the snipe to appear.

A percussionist may have to wait for twenty minutes just to play a few beats, but those beats have to be exact, and they have to be passionate and climactic. All that the epistles of Paul say a Christian should be—faithful, waiting, trusting, filled with fervor, hopeful—are the qualities of the good percussionist.

The other Lutheran instrument, of course, is the harp. It's made for a very nice person with strong forearms. You almost never see a harpist with a cigarette dangling out of her mouth. Having a harp is like living with an elderly parent in very poor health; it's hard to get them in and out of cars and hard to keep them happy. It takes hours to tune a harp, which remains in tune for about ten minutes or until somebody opens a door and lets in the cold air. It's an instrument for a saint.

If a harpist could find a good percussionist, they really wouldn't need an orchestra. They could settle down and make perfectly good music, just the two of them, as Lutherans have always done.

*One problem with twenty-four men on a twenty-six-foot boat is that in the Midwest we need to stand about twenty-eight inches or more from each other; otherwise, we get headaches.*

# 3

# Pontoon Boat

It has been a quiet week in Lake Wobegon. It's been hot and dry, and everyone was extremely touchy, so when you walked into the Chatterbox for lunch and sat at the counter and got your cup of coffee and looked at the menu and finally ordered what you have every day anyway—a bowl of chili and a grilled cheese—and turned to Ed on your left and were set to say something, you hesitated. Even to say, "Boy, she's a hot one," might start something. So you made it a question and asked, "Say, I wonder how hot she's supposed to get today anyway?" And he said, "How the hell should I know? What? You think I sit listening to the damn radio all morning?"

That's how hot it was. So hot you didn't dare ask, and no rain, but muggy so the dust sticks to your face. It doesn't seem fair for the Midwest, the nation's icebox, to be the nation's oven, too. It's like living in the Arctic but spending your summers at Death Valley. Even at the Sidetrack Tap, where men sit in air-cooled comfort in dim light and medicate themselves against anger and bitterness, they were touchy, too.

It's so good to step out of a hot dirty day into a cool tavern and hold a bottle of Wendy's, but two or three Wendy's later, it's so awful to go back out. After an hour in the dark, the sunlight hits you like a two-by-four, and the beer in your head heats up, the yeast grows, the brain rises. When a man on a hot day who's enjoyed an hour of fellowship gets up to leave, he knows he has dug a hole for himself.

The portly gent in the cool dark behind the bar, Wally, recently bought a boat, a twenty-six-foot pontoon boat with a green-striped canopy, a 36 hp outboard, four lawn chairs, and a barbecue grill, which arrived Sunday by flatbed truck and was put in the water off Art's fishing dock. It was christened the *Agnes D.* after his mother. He and his wife, Evelyn, took a maiden voyage in the twilight. It was cool out there under the canopy, with a nice breeze off the lake. Wally stood at the tiny wheel amidships, wearing a white skipper cap. His ship was only a piece of plywood, twenty-six by twelve, on two steel pontoons, but to him, standing, steering it, it was majestic. He wanted to hang lights on it from bow to stern, on port (left) and starboard (right) sides. He gunned it. "Not so fast," Evelyn said. "You don't have to drive the boat so fast."

"My love," he said, "you do not drive a boat. You drive a car. You sail a boat. And when you sail a boat, you need to find out what she's got under the hood." She'd never heard him talk like that.

He didn't talk like that in the Sidetrack—he didn't want anyone to think he was showing off—so when guys asked what was this they heard about him buying a boat, Wally frowned, shook his head, and said, "Yeah, I don't know. I got a deal on it from a guy I know, but I tell you, it's a headache. Insurance and the upkeep and worrying about the thing—did you know that if some fellows stole my boat to commit crimes with, and they got hurt, I could be liable? It's true! But you and the wife oughta come out with us some evening. Wouldn't that be something? We could grill up some steaks, have a beer. . . ."

He invited about a hundred couples aboard the *Agnes D.* in three days. An occupational hazard of being a tavern owner is that you have an awful lot of extremely close friends, men who've become very intimate and told you confidential things they wouldn't even tell their close friends. That makes you their closest friend, although you barely know their names.

When he invited Mayor Clint Bunsen to come for a cruise, Clint said, "You know what you ought to do? There's a bunch of Lutheran ministers coming through on a tour Friday. We oughta give them a boat ride so they get a nice look at town."

How and why twenty-four Lutheran ministers were touring rural Minnesota is a long digression that I'd rather skip, dear reader. People are so skeptical, they force a storyteller to spend too much time on the details and not enough on the moral, so I'll just say that the five-day tour, "Meeting the Pastoral Needs of Rural America," was organized by an old seminary pal of Pastor Ingqvist's, the Reverend J. Peter Larson, who called him in April and said, "You know what our problem is? We're so doggone theological we can't see past the principles to the people, and the people are hurting, so I'm organizing a tour of a hundred ministers to go and look at rural problems, and I want to visit Lake Wobegon in mid-July."

"Fine," said David Ingqvist, who forgot about it until last Sunday, when his wife, Judy, said, "What's this on the calendar for Friday? 'Tour/Larson here'?"

"Oh, that," he said. "Well," he said, "I was meaning to discuss that with you," he said. "It's some Lutheran ministers coming through town, and I thought we could have them over for a picnic supper in the backyard."

"How many?" she asked.

"I don't know exactly, but certainly no more than a hundred."

"Well, I think your best bet would be wieners. You probably just want to boil them. Maybe you could get someone to make you some potato salad."

Rural problems were what Pete wanted to see, but you can't take a crowd of ministers around to someone's house and point to him and say, "There's one. He's in trouble. I don't give him long. No, sir. He's headed down the chute." Clint Bunsen thought it was strange. If a minister visits, you hide your problems and shine up your children and put them through their paces. And you talk about other people's problems. But he agreed to talk to them about municipal affairs, and then he got the brilliant idea of the boat trip. When they arrived, tired and hot and dusty at five o'clock on Thursday, that was the plan: boat trip, speech on board and roasted wienies, and fellowship at the Ingqvists' (four gallons of wine, $4.39 apiece).

They got off the bus, and Clint thought, *Ministers*. Men in their forties mostly, a little thick around the middle, thin on top, puffy hair around the ears, some fish medallions, turtleneck pullovers, earth tones, Hush Puppies. But more than dress, what set them apart was the ministerial eagerness, more eye contact than you were really looking for, a longer handshake, and a little more affirmation than you needed. "Good to see you, glad you could be here, nice of you to come, we're very honored," they said to him, although they were guests and he was the host.

"Down this way! Let's go! Down to the lake!" Pastor Ingqvist wore yellow Bermuda shorts and sunglasses.

"It's been an incredible trip," Pete said. "Really amazing."

They strolled down from Bunsen Motors, down the alley behind Ralph's, and along the path between Mrs. Mueller's yard and Elmer and Myrtle's. Myrtle's cat lay on the limb of an apple tree, its long gray tail hanging down and twitching at the tip. Mrs. Mueller's cat sat in the shade of an old green lawn chair, its gaze set on the birdbath.

"I tell you," Pete said, "I really feel we've gotten an affirmation of Midwestern small-town values as something that's tremendously viable in people's lives. But there's a dichotomy between the values and the politics that is really critical at this point. It's a fascinating subject."

Wally had gone all out. The *Agnes D.* was hung with two strings of Christmas lights, the kind that twinkle on and off. He had laid in five cases of pop, a keg of beer, and enough frankfurters to feed the freshman class. The twenty-four men trooped up the plank and on deck, and she sank lower and lower in the water. Clint was the last aboard. He thought, *I'm not sure about this.* But how do you tell some ministers to get off? The church invites us all; the concept of "That's enough for now" isn't part of Lutheran teaching, so Clint stepped lightly aboard, trying not to put all his weight on the deck, and felt water slosh in his shoe.

The boat was riding low, no doubt about it. Wally thought, *I'm not sure about this,* but he didn't want to sound worried like an amateur. A true sailor would be hearty. He yelled, "Cast off the bowline!" Pastor Ingqvist leaned over to cast off, and the *Agnes D.* tilted to starboard. Wally gunned the engine, she righted herself, and off they went at about 4 mph, with little waves lapping at the sides, so low in the water that to people onshore it looked like a miracle.

One problem with twenty-four men on a twenty-six-foot boat is that in the Midwest we need to stand about twenty-eight inches or more from each other; otherwise, we get headaches. With the steering post, lawn chairs, motor, canopy, pop cases, barbecue grill, and card table, there wasn't room. Men herded forward and to the sides; there was a clearing of throats and a mumbling of "Excuse me's" as twenty-four men edged away from each other and into each other, and that was before the coals got hot.

Wally poured half a can of lighter fluid on the coals and lit them just before departure. As the heat rose, ministers standing near the grill edged away toward the bow. There were too many Lutherans squeezed into too small a space, and with the barbecue shooting up sparks and men ducking and edging, Wally thought, *If we'd just get up more speed, I'll bet that bow would come up a little.*

Pete was saying to Pastor Ingqvist, "Dave, I don't have the answers, but I think that all of us will come out of this with a feeling of unity of concern," but David was feeling his own concern: they were sinking and he didn't know how to mention it in a way that wouldn't seem negative. Wally stood at the wheel, calling, "Steady as she goes!" and twenty-four nervous ministers in earth tones and suede shoes were edging, shifting, herding, trying to be good listeners and share concerns as the fire got hotter and hotter, driving them toward the bow, which was sinking, but all of them were trying to keep a good positive attitude, and then Dave said, "Somebody put out the fire! We're sinking!"

Five men took their beer cups and leaned over to dip up water—and the *Agnes D.* tipped. The front left pontoon went under and the *Agnes D.* stopped dead in the water and turned to port. They had reached the edge of the laws of physics. The men lurched to the starboard side, and both pontoons went under. There in full view of town, the boat pitched forward and dumped some ballast: eight Lutheran ministers in full informal garb took their step for total immersion.

As the boat sank, they slipped over the edge to give their lives for Christ, but in only five feet of water. It's been a hot, dry summer.

Eight went over, and then the *Agnes D.* came up again a little, and the survivors grabbed to hold on, but then the grill tipped over and they turned to see hundreds of burning coals sliding down the deck toward them—the Book of Revelation come to life!—and they plunged overboard like a load of hay bales. The *Agnes D.*'s bow rose, and Wally turned to Clint, who was hanging on to the canopy, and said, "I think I got her under control now."

The ministers stood perfectly still in the water and didn't say much at all. Five feet of water, and some of them not six feet tall, so their faces were upraised to the bright blue sky. They didn't dare walk for fear of drop-offs, their clothes were too heavy to swim in, and they couldn't call for help because their voices were too deep and mellow. So they stood, faces upturned, in prayerful apprehension. Twenty-four ministers standing up to their smiles in water, chins up, trying to understand this experience and its deeper meaning.

Clint's little nephew Brian waded out to them. "It's not deep this way," he said. He stood about fifteen feet away, a little boy up to his waist. They followed him out single file, twenty-four dripping clergy, their clothes hanging heavy as millstones, but still looking interested, concerned, eager to get on to the next item on the agenda. It was fellowship at Pastor Ingqvist's home, but he was still aboard the *Agnes D.* with Wally and Clint, so they sat down in a circle under the trees to await further directions.

*You have to try. That's the Lutheran philosophy.*
*You can only do so much, and you have to try to do at least that.*

4

PK

It has been a quiet week in Lake Wobegon. It's been three days of summer and three of fall, and last night a cold rain fell, which makes almost everyone in my town a little more cheerful.

The sophomore class of Lake Wobegon High got on a bus and rode to the Cities on Tuesday to visit the zoo and the university farm campus and downtown Minneapolis to watch the trading on the floor of the Water Exchange. Minnesota is a major producer of mineral water, you know, and about a million gallons of water change hands every day at the Water Exchange. The class filed very quietly through the zoo, looking at tigers and dolphins and fabulous birds and primates, and at each stop, when the docent asked, "Are there any questions?" none of the kids said a word. At the farm campus, a professor of dairy husbandry took them through the barns and then showed them a prototype of a new milking machine developed to milk cats. Cats used to be kept as dairy animals, he said, because it was believed that their milk gave people courage, an essential element in life, but in the end, milking a cat was too labor intensive: you'd work half the morning with your thumbs and forefingers, and of course the cat didn't appreciate it, so it took another person to hold the cat, and gradually people gave up on cat's milk, figuring they could get their courage elsewhere. Some people felt that courage had only served to get them into trouble, and they preferred caution, but now, thanks to digital technology, a machine could provide the precise gentle suction needed to take a cat's milk, and there was, he said, a great market for this in Japan and Malaysia, and eventually here. Cat's milk, he said, was now used by several NFL teams, including Cincinnati and Detroit, and they found that linemen, after two weeks of cat's milk, would run head-on into concrete walls. He asked for questions. There were none.

They got on the bus for the long ride home. Forty kids and four adults, including Judy Ingqvist, whose daughter, Katherine, is a sophomore. Judy sat in the front of the bus with the other adults, a decent thing for chaperones to do. Keep your back to them. Three years ago, Judy led a bloody campaign to get the school board to pay parents who served as chaperones. The board was horrified and talked about the spirit of volunteering, and Judy talked about how money is tight in most families and the supply of volunteers is dwindling and minding children is hard work and people ought to be trained for it and get paid. Judy lost. So she has felt obligated to volunteer since then. And also, she thought she might find material for a poem. *Lutheran Vision* magazine has a poetry contest for ministers' wives, and first prize is five hundred dollars. Five hundred dollars would help the Ingqvists pay for a January trip to Hawaii, which they would love to take. So Judy sat with her notepad on the bus, and Marilyn Hedlund, the other chaperone, sat next to her, and in front of them sat Miss O'Brien and Mr. Bannister, the teachers. Bannister had said to Judy at the zoo, "This sure is a well-behaved group," and she wanted to hit him. "I believe the word is *cowed*," she said. Bannister was a complete zero. Miss O'Brien wasn't much better. She had no gumption. She was like the kids. She seemed to think that if she was just quiet and smiled, she'd be able to stay out of trouble and people would like her.

Judy's daughter, Kate, is getting to be that way. Judy is afraid for her. She's tall and blond, like her father, and she's lovely, but in the past year, Judy has seen a change in her. Kate isn't doing as well in school, she gave up soccer, and she begged her parents to let her cash in a savings bond so she could send off to a mail-order house in Los Angeles and buy a certain baby blue angora sweater for $285 that she absolutely needed to get. Those fuzzy angora sweaters Judy remembers from high school as having been worn by all the dumbest girls she knew. Kate needed the sweater because she had been admitted to the most exclusive group in Lake Wobegon High School. It's called the Do-Rites and goes back thirty years, a sorority of twelve girls—Kate was the only sophomore girl tapped for membership—and every spring at the school talent show, as the finale, the Do-Rites come out in their identical black skirts, black tights, high-heeled pumps, and angora sweaters and perform "To Know, Know, Know Him Is to Love, Love, Love Him" and "Da Doo Ron Ron." They sing the songs perfectly, every syllable, every chord, and do the steps with a precision that makes the crowd gasp—because they have rehearsed them for hours every week all year. To achieve five minutes of pure perfection is the purpose of the Do-Rites. They work all year for it, doing their hair, doing their skin, learning the songs, learning the steps, getting their outfits together. To Judy Ingqvist, a born feminist, the Do-Rites are like a Satanic cult. She hears the tape deck in Kate's bedroom playing the damned songs, hears Kate in her stocking feet doing the routines over and over, and she wants to scream. To bring up your child to be a Gloria Steinem or a Carol Bly and then wake up one morning to find Sandra Dee is exquisite misery.

"I don't know if I can make it through the winter," Judy said to her husband, the father of Sandra Dee, one night.

"You don't like 'To Know, Know, Know Him Is to Love, Love, Love Him and I Do'?" he asked.

She said, "The Do-Rites are so sick—it's like girls applying for admission to prison. It's like boot camp for bimbos."

"Oh," he said. "It'll pass."

"Sure," she said. "That's what people used to say about typhoid."

Kate is a lovely person. She has a good heart. Growing up as the daughter of a Lutheran minister is surely hard in all sorts of ways, but it does let you see real life up close. Into your living room come strangers who are blissfully happy and strangers in deep distress. Young couples who hold hands continuously as if they draw oxygen from each other. They want to get married, and they do. And then there are young couples with their first babies, the sacred babies. Later babies the parents will be matter-of-fact about, almost as if they arrived by mail order, but the first baby is like a little Buddha, sitting solemnly, beautifully dressed, venerated by its parents, who prostrate themselves before this tiny deity. A pastor's living room also gets people who are over-whelmed when their life suddenly for no reason breaks down, nothing works anymore, and nothing seems pleasant or funny—there is just a hellish meanness and darkness and pain. The pastor's child sees this. Lutherans are such stoics, they don't go to the pastor until it's really horrible, and the pastor's child opens the door and sees those people, their hollow eyes, their strange voices, as if they have broken glass in their mouths. And a pastor's child sees death. A dear father is dead, or a mother is gone, and the family is stunned, and the pastor's child sits politely and watches them weep: the women, how beautifully they sob, and how awkward are the men, who have less practice and don't let the tears down easily. Women sing as they weep—they weep like cellos playing a slow movement of Bach—and men sit, holding it in, as if they are sick to their stomachs, and then sobs erupt from them like barks, like the terrible honks of someone just learning to play trombone.

A pastor's child learns that you treat all of these people with the same quiet kindness: you offer congratulations to some and condolences to others, but you say it in the same kind voice, not interfering with people's feelings or trying to analyze them, offering the simplest comfort of a hand and a voice, the presence of another human being, here in their extreme moment. And you bring a hotdish.

Kate came home from school last week and said, "I'm changing my name to Kathy."

Judy did not look up from the sink. "Oh," she said.

"I just think it's nicer," said Kate.

"Well, it's up to you," said Judy.

It broke her heart, but she bit her lip and said nothing. Kathy is a nice name, but why wouldn't any girl rather be a Kate if she could be a Kate?

Judy thought, *This is my fault. I've been too loud, too pushy. I haven't comforted my daughter, and so she has turned for comfort to a drill team for dummies.*

Judy thought, *No, I haven't been loud enough. These kids are drifting. They're sleepwalking. We cheated them. We gave them television, that hypnotic glow, and they float along watching it, and now they float along on the Internet, and they discover the pleasures of being dumb and listless. The great literature, the great music that our parents thrust upon us and that threw us into dark waters of thought and feeling that we had to learn to swim in . . . But these kids grow up passive and illiterate—probably a third of these kids can't read well enough to enjoy doing it, and in another ten years, it'll be two-thirds. A person ought to protest this,* she thought.

She thought, *I ought to shave my head. A biblical sign of grief. Why not? Shave my head and challenge people to ask me why I did it. And if they asked, I'd tell them, "Because I'm angry about what's happening to our children."*

And then she leaned forward and said to the bus driver, "Would you mind stopping up there at the top of that hill?" He did. Judy stood up. She turned around and smiled at all the children riding along in their private worlds, many of them with private sound systems clamped to their heads. She said, "This has been such a fine day with all of you, I thought we should stop for just a minute and think about what we've seen together—the city, the people, the animals. I feel such energy in this group; you're wonderful kids, and here we are on this absolutely beautiful fall day with all the colors, and why don't we share a moment together and sing 'America the Beautiful'?" And she started singing and they joined right in—the spacious skies and the amber waves of grain—and there were the spacious skies and amber cornfields around them. Some of the kids liked singing it. The bus driver sang. He even wept. Later she found out he was drunk. But her daughter, Kathy, sat with her eyes on the floor and barely moved her mouth.

Well, you have to try. That's the Lutheran philosophy. You can only do so much, and you have to try to do at least that. You offer people a hand and a voice. Let them know you're there. It almost doesn't matter what you say. Just be there.

*Ernie said he sat and watched birds for hours, and then one day
a bird landed on his shoulder and he felt it was God's blessing him
in some mysterious way he could not understand but could only accept.*

# 5

# Gospel Birds

It has been a quiet week in Lake Wobegon. Lyle got a new car on Monday. Got it in St. Cloud, which didn't make him too popular. They say, "You want to buy a car in St. Cloud, fine, then you'll be able to drive your kids to school there, too." It's a little red foreign car, a sort of car not sold in Lake Wobegon; it has a sunroof that cranks back, which there isn't a great call for up here—people drive, they want a solid roof over their heads. But Lyle saw it in an ad and it took his breath away—a photograph on a dazzling summer day, looking down through the sunroof at the driver, a girl in a bathing suit barely big enough to be called a garment. Lyle is forty and suffers from foolish thoughts, more of them than he had when he was young and foolish. So he bought the car. When it didn't start for him on Tuesday morning, at least ten people sitting down to breakfast up and down McKinley Street looked at each other and smiled. Including the one who put the potato up the tailpipe.

Lyle is a newcomer to town, having lived here only twelve years, and I guess he doesn't know you're supposed to buy from your own, not go to strangers. This applies to the purchase of automobiles and to other forms of romance. A forty-year-old man who gets a crush on a girl in a magazine is not operating with his clutch fully engaged, as they say.

One Sunday morning, Lyle got in line to go forward to receive Communion, and his eye fell on a handsome young woman ahead of him in line. By the time he reached the front, his heart was in no condition to take Communion, and he was in a condition that made him embarrassed to turn around and go back to his seat. He plopped down in the front pew and assumed a prayerful attitude that was more for camouflage than for devotion, and remained there until the crisis passed.

Now he is gadding about town in a little red foreign car that obviously was meant for someone else and not a high school science teacher with a wife and four children. Carl took him aside the other day and said, "Lyle, it's none of my business what you do, but I ask this as a personal favor: please don't get a permanent and please don't grow a mustache." Lyle hadn't considered either one before, and he's thought of both a lot since. Poor man, what he needs to do is lose weight. That car lists to the left when he's in it. He's carrying about fifty pounds more than he was designed for.

Twelve years in a town and still a stranger, poor man. Maybe all he needs is a little friendship and affection. There is some of that around, but it's old friendship and old affection, and you have to live here a long time in order to recognize it, because it's unspoken. One day last winter I was in the Sidetrack Tap playing pinball; they have the old machines that keep scores in the hundreds and the thousands, not the hundred thousands, and make dinging sounds, not beeps, and I was making it ring pretty well and was up to four thousand when the machine ate the ball, and then I felt Carl Krebsbach's hand on my shoulder. He'd been standing at my elbow, and he put his arm around me. I almost fainted. I know Carl well enough to know he doesn't go around doing that.

Lyle was in the Sidetrack this past week, and Wally just gave him a hard time. Twelve years and he still gets picked on by the bartender. He looked at Lyle and said, "What do you want?" Other guys he doesn't ask; he knows what they want. "What do you want?" he said.

Wally subscribes to the *Tavern Owners Monthly*, the *Tom-Tom*, a little newsletter, and in the October issue, which arrived late because Mr. Bauser at the post office has a sore wrist, Wally read an article about a guy who went into a tavern in southern Minnesota, had a couple of beers, got in his car, drove into a tree, and sued the tavern for $4,000—half for damages to the car, half for mental anguish—and collected. Wally couldn't believe it. Whatever happened to paying for your mistakes? What happened to learning the hard way? Accepting responsibility?

Then in walks Lyle. Wally looked at him, thought, *Ja, that's the guy who'd do it to me.*

Lyle says, "A Leinie."

Wally says, "Okay, but just one."

Lyle says, "How come just one?"

Wally says, "Because you don't look good to me."

"What's the matter? What'd I do?"

"It's not what you done; it's what you might do. One. That's it."

The highlight of this week was not Lyle and his new car, though, but the performance at Lake Wobegon Lutheran on Wednesday night of Ernie and Irma Lundeen and their Performing Gospel Birds. The deacons voted last summer to put on some Wednesday night programs because Wednesday night prayer meeting and Bible reading have not been drawing well; some nights only five or six people show up, and if Pastor Ingqvist isn't one of them, they look at each other and think, *Well? What do we do now?* and maybe have silent prayer and sit for a while and just read. Val Tollefson was the one who pushed the idea of programs, and he wrote to a Christian booking agency, and so, coming up in the months ahead are Brother Flem Hospers, the world's tallest evangelist, and the Singing Whipples, who play among the six of them thirty-seven musical instruments, and in February the regional play-offs in Scripture drill competition, and in the spring Rev. Duke Peterson, former runner-up Mr. Minnesota and champion weight lifter whose use of bodybuilding drugs reduced him to the level of a wild animal and almost led to his death—he was dead for six and a half minutes and saw visions of the other side, but then he was revived and entered the ministry. And on Wednesday night, Ernie and Irma and the Performing Gospel Birds. Pastor Ingqvist did not attend; he had pressing business elsewhere—wherever he could find it, I guess. He said to everyone who asked, "This was not my idea. This is Val Tollefson's project. Ask Val about it."

Now, the Lutherans of Lake Wobegon are a dignified bunch, and to hear them talk after Sunday service, you wouldn't think anyone was going to see the birds, but as Wednesday night rolled around, people thought they might if they had time go up to the church just to see what it was. And of course, Wednesday night being the sort of night it is in Lake Wobegon, almost everyone did have time, and at 7:30 there they were in their seats, a little sheepish, and then Ernie and Irma walked out to the pulpit, each of them covered with birds— doves, canaries, parakeets, a couple of parrots, a crow—there must've been forty birds perched on them, and all the birds were singing at the tops of their voices. It was awesome. It was wonderful. A symphony of birds. So beautiful. Then he bowed his head to pray and the birds were quiet. Not a peep. And it was a long prayer. Ernie prayed that those who had come to mock would have their hearts opened to the message. That made people feel pretty small.

The birds did some tricks: some did acrobatics and walked a tight-rope blindfolded, and the parrots talked—Scripture verses—and the canaries picked out a couple of hymns on a xylophone, which was nice. Ernie talked awhile about the wayward life they had led in the circus for many years performing under the name the Flying Lundinis, and meanwhile Irma was dressed as other animals walking two by two into the ark, and then from the back of the sanctuary—and who knows how it got back there—a dove swooped over their heads and circled the room three times. It descended on the ark, and the ark opened and all the birds rose from it in a cloud. It was good. Then the birds took up the collection—flew around and took the dollar bills out of your fingers on the fly and brought them forward—pretty exciting—and someone held up a fifty-cent piece, and a parakeet took that and lost altitude suddenly but somehow made it back to port.

It was about a forty-five-minute program, and everything in it was absolutely memorable. Ernie and Irma talked about when they were children, which was sad—they were poor and they were lonely, and that was how they came to love birds; birds were so lovely and grace-ful and free. Ernie said he sat and watched birds for hours, and then one day a bird landed on his shoulder and he felt it was God's blessing him in some mysterious way he could not understand but could only accept. For God's eye is the sparrow; God knows if a sparrow falls, so we know that God is watching over us. And then four parakeets picked out that hymn on tiny silver bells: "I sing because I'm happy.

I sing because I'm free. For his eye is on the sparrow. And I know he watches me." It was lovely. Two-part harmony.

And then Ernie said, "And now, to close our program, I'd like you to feel that same thrill I felt when the bird landed on my shoulder. I'd like every head bowed and every eye closed as all of us contemplate God's great love in our lives, and when the bird comes to you and lands on your shoulder, if you feel that special blessing in your heart, I'd ask you to stand at your seat. You don't need to come forward. Just stand where you are. And now, the Blessing of the Birds."

The Lutherans of Lake Wobegon are a very reserved bunch, I'd have you know, and though they had often closed their eyes and meditated in church before, it lent a certain excitement to meditation to close your eyes knowing that a bird was about to land on you and wondering which one. Minutes passed in silence as people got down to the business of meditation and thoughts of divine providence came to mind—ways in which their lives had been supported and upheld by powerful love outside themselves; powerful evil resisted despite the desire to follow it; acts of love and kindness they had felt called to despite embarrassment; and more than that, a presence of grace in the world that is almost beyond our comprehension—and then they heard a rush of wings as if angels were in the room, and one by one felt a light weight on their shoulders as if someone tapped them, and one by one stood, eyes closed, and felt not only touched by this but filled somehow. They were stunned, especially the ones who had come to be amused and make fun of the performance. Something had happened; they weren't sure what, but something. Everyone agreed that it had been a mysterious experience.

Lyle wasn't there. Maybe as a science teacher he'd know so much about conditioned response that it would have no effect on him—I don't know. I wish I had been there. All this month, as I see flocks of our summer birds head south, I feel sad. Now I feel a little happier, having told you the story of Ernie and Irma Lundeen and the Performing Gospel Birds, but if I had been there, I'm sure I would have told it even better.

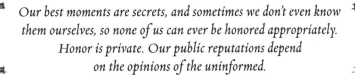

*Our best moments are secrets, and sometimes we don't even know them ourselves, so none of us can ever be honored appropriately. Honor is private. Our public reputations depend on the opinions of the uninformed.*

# 6

# Twentieth Anniversary

It rained this week, rained all day on Wednesday, and the trees lost a lot of leaves, and now the town divides into the raking and non-raking factions. Most are rakers, but a few hold to the position that leaves are fertilizer and should be left where they are. It was warm on Friday and the sun shone, and it was just a lovely fall day, piles of golden leaves everywhere, and of course with the leaves off them you get a better look at the trees, and the smell in the air was like red wine. Unfortunately, the people of Lake Wobegon are not wine drinkers, so they don't know what they have.

A flock of geese went over town on Friday heading north, an interesting sight. People were watching for them today, hoping that the geese might have stopped during the night and discussed it and voted in new leadership, but why should they be smarter than anyone else? They do have only the sense that God gave geese.

If you had been hiking out in the woods, up behind the high school, up the hill, you might have come across Pastor Ingqvist collecting leaves. He had a paper bag full, which he carried so that if anyone came along he would have a reason for being up there. Men in Lake Wobegon do not simply hang out in the woods for the sheer experience; you have to have a motive. This is what makes most men hunters. They want to be in the woods, but they need a reason.

Pastor Ingqvist was up walking around in the woods because he was depressed. This summer, the church board did not give him a salary increase, on the grounds that he had not asked for one, which was true—he hadn't—but the reason he hadn't was that he thought it was obvious that he should have one. It's been five years since the last raise, and that one was a tiny symbolic raise. "Why don't you ask for a raise?" asked his wife, Judy. "This is your twentieth anniversary serving this church." Well, he didn't ask because money is something you don't talk about in this town. Money is unmentionable. You stick out a twenty-dollar bill toward a Lake Wobegonian, and he'll recoil as if you'd given him a soggy Kleenex—no, thank you. We're country people, and in the country, if someone needs your help you give it to him, and he does the same for you someday. We don't wave money at each other. Money is an ugly subject to us. The school board feels this way every time the teachers' contract comes up, that a sacred profession such as teaching should not be dragged down by associating it with money.

So they continued him at the same salary, but the board did name a committee to honor the pastor on his twentieth anniversary. It included some of the drowsiest people in the church, and they decided that, instead of doing as other congregations have so often done—sending the minister and his lovely wife on a trip to Greece, perhaps purchasing a late-model car—they would publish a few of the pastor's sermons in a small, ugly, commemorative booklet. They wanted it to be a surprise, so they didn't ask him to select the sermons. They chose their own favorites, and so, at the service last Sunday, during announcements, Val Tollefson rose and congratulated the pastor and handed him a copy. It was a hundred pages, expensively bound, with a real leather cover, padded leather, a sort of livid brown the color of a diseased liver with silver spackled onto it to represent the Milky Way, evidently, and it was entitled *To Know Him Is to Love Him*, which he immediately recognized as the title of one of the dumbest sermons he ever gave, and there it was in silver lettering, eternalized. He opened the book and his heart sank: there was a dopey picture of him looking pompous and full of gas, and an illiterate introduction by Val himself. Val is a writer who likes to put words in quotation marks. His essay begins, "It's an honor for me personally to be asked to 'say a few words' about Pastor David Ingqvist, or 'Dave,' as we know him, and yet when I sit down to 'put pen to paper,' I find that the proverbial cat has 'got my tongue' and I wish, as our Lord once so aptly put it, that this cup would pass from me." He went on in this dithery vein for a few pages. Eighty pages of sermons followed on glossy paper, expensive, and one glance at them showed him that out of hundreds of sermons they had gone straight for the ones he'd been trying to forget. Those dismal dumb sermons that ought to be followed by a prayer for forgiveness. Those big, pretentious, overwritten sermons that make you grateful for all the people who weren't in church that day.

Afterward, during coffee hour, people came around to shake his hand and congratulate him, and the poor minister and his wife stood in ashen silence. The booklet must have cost a couple thousand dollars easily—something so ugly doesn't come cheap. A couple thousand would've been a nice salary increase, or it would've bought a trip—a couple thousand dollars could've meant something, but instead they threw it down this rat hole of a commemorative booklet.

"To Know Him Is to Love Him" was a sermon he gave after he and Judy came back from a trip to Minneapolis five years ago. They were so broke that year, Minneapolis was the only place they could afford to go for a vacation. People from Lake Wobegon view Minneapolis as a cesspool of crime and degradation where no person in his right mind would walk down the street unless he was with three friends armed with deer rifles. You can't trust anybody there, and nobody in their right mind would ever go there, because you'd never find a job or make friends or meet a decent woman or be able to raise a family. People in Lake Wobegon watch the evening news on TV, and nothing that happens in Russia or Somalia or Bosnia interests them so much as one drive-by shooting in Minneapolis. That's what they watch the news for. Every murder in Minneapolis is one more justification for their decision after high school to stay put and not head for the big city. In the Sidetrack Tap, they pay no attention to the news except when there's a story about crime in Minneapolis, and then the bar is silent. People soak up the details of the story: she was alone, in the parking ramp; it was four o'clock in the afternoon. And they look at each other. Four o'clock in the afternoon. Four o'clock in the afternoon. I don't know. People down there. Why would you live there? They don't have anything down there that we don't have here—we got the same houses, same cars, get the same TV shows—but out here we know who our neighbors are.

The sermon he gave was about a little incident that happened to them in downtown St. Paul. They were about to cross the street when a well-dressed woman pulled up to the crosswalk in a brand-new Mustang and stopped. The light was red for her, so the Ingqvists started across. But here in Minnesota we allow a right turn on a red light, so she looked to her left and saw no cars coming and started up and then looked ahead and saw two Lutherans splayed across her hood, and then she jammed on her brakes. The sermon was about the fact that she never got out of the car. She put her hands over her face, she gave them a horrified look, she gave them a look of apology, and she mouthed the words, "I'm sorry, I didn't see you," but she didn't get out of her car. She made the right turn. To almost kill somebody and then drive away—David thought this was the most callous thing anybody had ever done to him. He thought this pretty well typified the dehumanization in the world today, and he wrote a sermon about it. Unfortunately, his text that week had to do with the parable of the vineyard, and it was hard to get that car into the vineyard, and it turned out to be a whole lot of nothing. Like one of those big government buildings full of marble and pretentious bad taste. And now this sermon was entombed in this commemorative booklet. It made him wish that woman hadn't stopped. At least at your funeral, when people who didn't give a fig about you stand up and pay pretentious homage to all the most useless parts of your life, you don't have to listen to them.

How is it that people can honor you and make you feel so small?

David Ingqvist is a direct descendant of the first Lutheran pastor to come to Lake Wobegon, Pastor Leif Ingqvist and his wife, Anna. They had come over from Norway after the terrible herring famine and the awful schism in the Lutheran church of Stavanger, where the people divided over the question, "Will we recognize each other in heaven, or will our spiritual forms not have our earthly features?" The clergy fought this out for two years, some arguing, "Yes, of course we'll know Grandma there, and she will know us—the family was meant to be eternal," and other people saying, "No, we will go on to a finer and better life there, and if you think your face is anything God would allow in a place of perfect bliss, then you ought to take another look." People got all hot about it in that silent glacial way that Norwegians have, and the fight got so unpleasant that people would've gladly avoided heaven if it meant they'd have to talk to the others, and the Lutheran church split into the Facial and the Non-facial factions, and the Ingqvists were glad to leave. He did not know the answer to the personal recognition question, and it didn't interest him. He was happy to come to America, and he didn't feel homesick for Stavanger. The misery of this terrible argument cured him of all homesickness or regret. Norwegians are no fun to fight with because they do it silently: they know they're right, so why should they bother arguing about it? This can go on for years.

The Ingqvists came to Minnesota because they knew people here. Actually, their name was Nelson, Leif and Anna Nelson, but their English was poor and the immigration officer in New York asked so many questions, finally Leif turned to Anna and said something about it being like the Spanish Inquisition, and the immigration man wrote down "Ingqvist" and under nationality wrote "Spanish." So they became Ingqvists. By the time they learned English well enough to figure out how to change it back, they were used to it.

Pastor Leif and Anna Ingqvist came to Lake Wobegon in 1875 along with a Mr. and Mrs. Svendson. It was a cold winter, and the two couples shared a one-room log cabin that measured ten feet wide and fifteen feet long, and in the spring both of the women were pregnant. A great monument to civility, or to restraint. For a pastor and his wife to be able to accomplish this under the noses of the laity, and vice versa, has been an inspiration to clergy and laity in Lake Wobegon ever since.

Mrs. Svendson had a little girl whom they named Nissa, and Anna Ingqvist had twin boys named Einar and Ingmar. They were identical twins, and as they grew up they grew so identical that Leif would never call them by name. Being Norwegian, he did not ever want to be wrong about anything. He addressed them simply as "Son," and so did his wife, and eventually so did everyone else, and when, in 1885, one of the twins died in the flu epidemic, they didn't know which one it was, whether to bury Einar or Ingmar. They decided to put "Ingmar" on the tombstone, but for years thereafter they worried that maybe the wrong one was in the ground.

Einar grew up, but of course they never called him Einar, because he might be Ingmar, and he moved away to Minneapolis, to everyone's relief. If he was the dead one, then better he should go. Once he got to Minneapolis, he went into the publishing business and earned quite a bit of money publishing cheap romantic novels in Norwegian for the servant girl market. Novels in which blond men with powerful biceps held girls close to them and breathed on them.

One of the things that Pastor Leif Ingqvist had always preached against was fiction. Fiction and alcohol, he felt, led a Christian down the path toward self-delusion, and he did not compromise his views. Pastor Leif Ingqvist stood in the pulpit and said, "I will not speak with moderation. I am in earnest—I will not equivocate, I will not excuse, I will not retreat a single inch, and I will be heard. Wrong is wrong. Untrue is untrue. And if it didn't happen, it's wrong to say so, as wrong as it is to take a drink. The man who would write untruth is the man who would take whiskey, and the love of God is not in him."

So the father and the son didn't speak to each other for forty years. And when the son decided that maybe he ought to, it was too late. His father had been dead for two years. The son went out and got drunk in a Minneapolis bar, and he wept and decided he would spend two thousand dollars on a monument in his father's memory, to honor him, and by sheer chance, the man sitting next to him in the bar happened to know a sculptor, and so the deal was struck, and they drank a toast to it, and that's how Lake Wobegon got the statue of the Unknown Norwegian.

It arrived on a truck in 1938 and was set down in the little triangular park on Main Street, and it resembled nobody they'd ever known. It certainly didn't look like Leif Ingqvist. It was a handsome, noble youth pointing west, and underneath it said, "Kan Du Glemme Gan Lie Norge?" Or "Can You Forget Dear Old Norway?" But of course Norway isn't to the west unless you take the long way. And Leif Ingqvist was glad to forget old Norway. You get into an argument over something you don't care about with people who are that much angrier with you because you don't, an argument that won't end because people refuse to talk about it, and you'll be glad to get away—if you're a person who wants to live a life. And a man who can get his wife pregnant a few feet away from another couple doing the same is a man who wants to live a life. People say that those couples did that because they didn't want to have to listen to each other. That Norwegians in ecstasy sound like foghorns.

Our best moments are secrets, and sometimes we don't even know them ourselves, so none of us can ever be honored appropriately. Honor is private. Our public reputations depend on the opinions of the uninformed. Each one of us is a book reviewed by critics who only read the chapter headings and the jacket flap. We're all a mystery. We should all respect each other on that basis.

*Some people have a love of their fellow man in their hearts,
and others require a light anesthetic.*

# 7

# Deer Camp

It has been a quiet week in Lake Wobegon. We got some snow on Sunday, and it's been gray and overcast most of the week. In the Sidetrack Tap, they were talking about deer season, which started this morning. Guys planning to get out on Friday and set up their camps, get their hunting shack ready, build a fire, sit around and drink beer and tell stories. Friday night is the best time, the night before hunting, a lot more fun than the hunt itself. People go out hunting so they can have the night before the hunt, which, of course, wouldn't be as much fun if you only did the night before and then packed up and came home—then it wouldn't be the night before. It's the same with taking vacation trips. The anticipation of the trip is so wonderful that it almost makes up for the dreariness and disappointment of the trip itself.

Daryl Tollerud and Roger Hedlund and Carl Krebsbach and Carl's brother-in-law Lowell from Minneapolis all headed off to Carl's hunting shack yesterday. It's up near Sigurd, Minnesota, up in a forest of scrub pine and popple, and it's a classic hunting shack—a zero-maintenance structure. You open the door and hear little feet scurrying away, and you walk in and sweep the floor and take the mattresses down from where they're hanging over the rafters and put 'em on the bunk beds and prime the pump and build a fire in the stove and get the whiskey out and the sausage and the eggs and the bread and the beer and go outside and stand, and there's one reason to go hunting right there—the chance to pee outdoors. An important ritual for men. Months go by and you don't think about it, and then suddenly you have the opportunity and the need, and you have this wonderful feeling of freedom. And then you come inside and the shack is starting to heat up and the sausages are on and you have a beer and a bump and you feel a warm glow come over you. Some people have a love of their fellow man in their hearts, and others require a light anesthetic. And the four friends put the eggs and sausage on their plates and eat, and all is well with the world. Tomorrow may bring weariness and frustration, tramping around after the wily white-tail, and it'll rain and it may get cold, and you'll think of the great Armistice Day Blizzard of 1940 and all those deer hunters who died in the woods, but the night before the hunt, that's perfect.

Here's Daryl Tollerud, who goes for months without ever setting foot in the Sidetrack Tap, and yet he's had two jelly glasses of bourbon, and he's beaming in a way you haven't seen before. Daryl has been looking forward to this hunting trip ever since Marilyn went to Seattle in September with her sister Cheryl and came home after ten days all aglow and talking about what a wonderful time they'd had, how the two of them had talked and laughed and had a ball—which of course made Daryl feel bad. When someone you love tells about the most wonderful trip of her life and it happens to be the first one in years that she took without you, it does raise questions in a man's mind. And then the pictures came back from the developer. And here they were in a restaurant eating lobster, and here was the hike on the Olympic Peninsula, and here was the sailboat they went out on in Port Townsend, and here was the ferryboat over to Bainbridge Island, and there was a picture of Marilyn and Cheryl and two guys, their arms around the women's backs, the four of them grinning at the camera.

"Oh," she said, "I meant to tell you about that." She laughed. "That was so funny. Those guys. Oh boy. I never laughed so hard in my life."

"What was so funny?" he asked.

"I was going to take Cheryl's picture standing at the rail, and I was about to take it, and this guy came and said, 'Why don't you get in the picture—I'll take it,' so I stood next to Cheryl, and then this other guy came and said to the first guy, 'Go ahead, get in the picture—I'll take it,' so he stood between us, and then this woman came along and said, 'Go ahead, get in the picture—I'll take it,' and so he got in the picture, and we were all laughing—it was so silly. She took the picture, and they turned out to be real nice guys from Seattle, and they took us to this terrific restaurant, and we had a great time. Craig, there, he works for Boeing, and Brad is a teacher. Teaches creative writing."

"Oh," said Daryl. "Sounds nice."

"You don't have to be jealous," she said. "Oh, for goodness' sake. Why do you have to take it that way? You think if we were running around with two guys out there we'd take our pictures with 'em? You think we're that dumb?"

"So what you're saying is that the guys I ought to worry about are the ones who aren't in the picture?"

"Oh, for pity's sake."

It hurt him to see that picture. Why did she think it was a big joke? He'd taken care of the kids for practically two weeks so she could go off and have fun, and it would've been nice if she'd come home and not talked so much about how much fun she had.

Roger Hedlund has been looking forward to this hunting trip since he came home from the big Risk Takers rally in Minneapolis where thousands of Lutheran men took the vow to open up emotionally and express their feelings—he went home and told his wife how much he loved her, and that was nice, and then he said he thought it'd be a nice idea if, instead of him going deer hunting, the two of them went to Chicago, and she said, "Roger, I appreciate the things you said, and I love you, and I always have. But, Roger, I'm sort of in a different place right now, where I'm starting to enjoy my own company after all these years of raising a family, and I've been able to make some very good women friends, and that first weekend of November, we're planning to go to a spa near the Cities, the four of us."

So he went deer hunting.

They sat in the shack and drank, and Carl recited the Hunters' Creed: "Love that which is wild and free. Love it, and let it go, and if it loves you, it will come back, and if it doesn't, then go out and find it and kill it." They told stories about hunting, and about the time Byron Tollefson dragged the giant duck decoy out in the woods and put Jell-O out for deer bait and crawled into the decoy and waited, and they told about the old man who trained his dog to chase deer and tree them—he'd get the deer running so fast they'd go right up a tree, and the old man found out what an inconvenience that was. They told about Bruno the fishing dog and how they tried to make him a hunting dog and trained him to point and to flush, and they taught him everything except that firearms would be involved, so when he pointed and flushed a pheasant and a shotgun went off, Bruno took off for town and became a fishing dog again.

And Carl told his story about the Hansens' dog, who bit him in the leg, and how he trained that dog with the use of raw oysters.

And Lowell said, "The problem with dog stories and hunting stories is that they're just about one thing. A good story ought to touch on five different elements: religion, money, family relationships, sex, and mystery. For example: 'God,' said the banker's daughter. 'I'm pregnant. I wonder who did it.' There it is—everything in one story."

"Or how about this one," Daryl said. "The young priest went to visit the old priest for dinner one evening, and there he noticed that the old priest had a new housekeeper and she was very young and beautiful. The old priest introduced her as his niece. She fixed a wonderful dinner for them, and about halfway through, the old priest leaned over and said, 'Father, I can tell what you're thinking, and I just want you to know that there's nothing immoral between me and my niece.' A week later, the housekeeper came to the old priest and said, 'Father, I hate to say this, but I've looked all over the place and the good silver gravy ladle is missing. It's been missing ever since the young father came over for dinner.' The old priest said, 'Well, I'll take care of it. I'll write him a note.' And he wrote: 'Dear Father, It was so good to see you for dinner, and thank you for the good company. I must say, however, that our good silver gravy ladle is missing. I'm not saying that you took it, and I'm not saying that you didn't take it, but it's been missing ever since you left.' And the young priest wrote back: 'Dear Father, Thank you for the wonderful dinner, which I enjoyed very much. I must say that I am sorry about your missing gravy ladle. I'm not saying that you are sleeping with your housekeeper, and I'm not saying that you aren't sleeping with your housekeeper, but if you had been sleeping in your own bed, you would have found your gravy ladle.'

"Sex, money, religion, family relationships, and mystery," said Daryl.

Roger Hedlund said, "The five things that we Lutherans are missing, especially the first and the last." He was drunk, but then so were the others, so nobody minded his saying this. He looked at the fire in the stove. "I was brought up to look down on Catholics, but I'll tell you—they're more honest than us and always have been. Catholics have vows of chastity. Lutherans just make sure not to enjoy it too much. You get married because you want to make love, and at first you feel like you won a million dollars in the lottery, and then it turns out to be the Norwegian lottery, where you win a dollar a year for a million years. We love the teachings of Luther for their own sake but also because it gives us something to hit the Catholics over the head with. We look down on them, but we reserve our greatest cruelty for fellow Lutherans. We believe that to forgive is a divine quality, and so we don't attempt it personally. Anybody who achieves success we consider a traitor. We are a cold and arrogant and unpleasant people, if the truth be told, and why shouldn't it be?"

He stood up as if he were going to say more, and he swayed, and he sat down.

"Ha," said Carl. "You think Lutherans are unpleasant, you ought to know Catholics. We don't eat meat on Friday, but we might drink gin for breakfast. We're against abortion and we're in favor of electrocution. We preach against the love of money, but we bend the knee to those who have it. We consider funerals a festivity and a time to get drunk and dance, but weddings are such sad events we put them off as long as possible. If we should ever get into heaven, God must have some sense of humor."

He poured a little bourbon into each glass all around. "We've all been disappointed by love and by our fellow man, but one thing is as good now as it ever was, and that is a good night's sleep, gentlemen." And that bourbon he poured was still sitting in the glasses when they woke up this morning. It was almost nine. They could hear distant gunshots. They crawled out of their sleeping bags, and the taste of whiskey was in their mouths, and they went outside and stood against a tree for the great pleasure of manliness, and then they fixed coffee and eggs and sausage and had breakfast and put on their orange jackets and loaded their guns and moved out through the woods, single file, the four of them, heading for the stand.

*What else is having babies about if not taking a chance?*

# 8

# Thanksgiving

Thanksgiving was Thursday, a cold, gray, windy day, and the Thanksgiving service at the Lutheran church was packed, to Pastor Ingqvist's great surprise. He expected a small turnout, like last year's, and hadn't prepared a complete sermon, only a couple of index cards, one with a text from the Psalms and the other saying only "Conclusion." He sat thinking hard through the opening hymns. Halfway into the reading from Ecclesiastes, the fire siren went off two blocks away, and everyone who had left a turkey in the oven sat up straight in the pew and had a vision of flames engulfing their home and the roof collapsing in a shower of sparks. All the firefighters jumped up and left and came back a minute later; it was nothing. Bud had accidentally jostled the siren switch while reaching back into the joists for something. Time for the sermon. It was a nervous and turbulent sermon, he felt, with a bumpy landing due to the loss of one engine, but afterward people shook his hand and said it was one of the finest they ever heard. "Beautiful. Do you have a transcript of that?" some people asked.

He thought, *You've got to be kidding*, but the Lutherans of Lake Wobegon don't use much irony, like they don't use much curry powder: some, not a lot. There stood the tall, slope-shouldered pastor in humiliation for a performance that one person after another said was wonderful, even Val Tollefson. "Well, I wish I'd prepared more, and tried to develop it a little better," he said, blushing, and thought, *Thank you, Lord, very much. Tusind takk, Lord.*

47

Clarence Bunsen wasn't in church. Arlene went, but the mister stayed home, because he wasn't very thankful. He got up that morning and stepped on a screw and tried to levitate off it and strained his back. His back didn't go out, but it felt weak. He didn't want to slip in the bathtub, so he took a bath instead of a shower and felt like an old vet at the Vets' Hospital, and climbing out he slipped and strained his back again, another part. While he was combing his hair, a clump came out, from the bunch that he's been combing across the top in hopes it would take hold. He came down to the kitchen feeling that life had turned against him.

Arlene said, "Have a cup of coffee. That'll perk you up, and usually that's all a Norwegian needs." Norwegians have often been revived by this method, including some whose EKG showed a flat line—a sip of coffee on their lips and the pen jumped. Clarence felt like coffee wouldn't make much difference.

He didn't tell Arlene that he'd talked to their daughter, Barbara Ann, on the phone Wednesday night. She was going on and on about this, that, and the other thing, and suddenly he had a premonition that the real reason she was coming home for Thanksgiving was to make an important announcement—of her divorce. She and Bill, married for ten years, the poor thing. He could understand; he always knew that Bill wasn't good for her. He didn't have Barbara Ann's undying enthusiasm; he was too serious, worked too hard, and earned far too much money. Clarence could understand her unhappiness—not that she said anything. She didn't. It was what she didn't say. He wanted to stay home from church and be alone.

One other thing: one day in October, Arlene had said, "How about we go to Minneapolis for Thanksgiving and stay at the Curtis and have the buffet in the Cardinal Room? I hear it's fabulous." And Clarence said, "Naw, let's stay home. If you're tired of making dinner, I'll do it." He heard himself say these words and heard her say, "Fine. Good. We'll stay home, and you make the dinner." One more reason he didn't go to church. Another was his fireplace, recently repaired by a man from Los Angeles named Curtis Olson. Byron Tollefson recommended him as a man who knew about fireplaces and chimneys, but when Olson left, Byron said, "No, I was only repeating what others had said. I forget who they were, but they said he was pretty good." Clarence didn't want to see Byron for a while, and Byron would be at church.

Olson came with full-color brochures about fireplace inserts and how for a low sum you could have a liner put in the chimney, guarding against chimney fire *and* improving the efficiency of fireplace and furnace by 50 to 70 percent. He installed a unit at Clarence's, and suddenly a fireplace that had worked pretty well started to go to hell. Smoke poured out into the living room, and the heat went up the chimney. Olson looked anguished. He paced up and down, wringing his hands, and said, "This is terrible; I didn't know your house had a problem with convex airflow. You have an inverse ratio—weren't you aware of it? *I* don't live here, it isn't my house, you couldn't expect *me* to know about your convexity problem. Now look, I've gone and made a mistake, walked into a minefield, and what am I going to do about it? I feel miserable. I came in here feeling good about myself, and in two days you've managed to completely destroy my confidence."

Clarence said, "I'm sorry you feel so bad. Why don't I have Carl come and look at it?"

"Well, all right," said Olson, "but I still feel like you don't have respect for me."

"No," said Clarence. "No, not at all."

Carl came and looked down the chimney. He said, "Whoever was here knocked some bricks loose, and he had to pound harder to get the liner in, so now you've got a wad of sheet metal stuck in there tight; I don't know if it's going to come out or not."

Olson called from Minneapolis. "I'm too upset to work right now," he said. "I feel threatened and embarrassed. I need some time alone." And there was seven hundred dollars gone, *click.*

Thanksgiving morning, Clarence built a small fire in the fireplace with an electric fan on the hearth to push the smoke up the chimney. He heard the door open, and a familiar voice said, "Hi, Daddy," and there she was: tall, lovely. He put his arms around her and had to go to the kitchen. Norwegian men cry privately and dab cold coffee on their eyes to get the redness out. Poor child. Thirty-four, about to be alone in the world.

"Can I help, Dad?" asked Bill, roaming into the kitchen.

"No, of course not. Fix yourself a drink."

"What do you have?"

"I don't know. It's in the basement."

"Care for something yourself?"

"No, I can't drink while I'm cooking."

He cooked. Basted the turkey, boiled yams, peeled potatoes, checked the pumpkin pie in the oven—thirty minutes, forty, forty-five, an hour—still it wasn't done. Then the crust caught on fire. He chipped off that part. The house smelled of smoke, but he was doing pretty well. That's what Arlene said, too, as she cruised through from time to time: "You're doing awfully well, dear. I'm proud of you. Are you boiling these potatoes here? Then you probably want to put some water in the pot—ah, the turkey smells good. Mmmmm. Want me to put some aluminum over it? It's up to you, but in a four-hundred-degree oven it might scorch after a while."

It was hard but far from impossible, and it felt good to cook and be in charge and not sit, as he had for years, in the living room with a silent son-in-law, saying, "Well, Bill, how's the real-estate business?" "Oh, not bad." Well, that took care of fifteen seconds; a couple hours more and we can wrap it up. He cooked and cooked, waiting for the news to drop, rehearsing his calm reaction. ("Well, kids, that's your decision. I can't say that I approve, but I certainly can sympathize. Arlene and I have been together for forty years, but there have been times . . .")

Then she told him. She said, "We have an announcement. We're going to have a baby. In April."

He almost said, "Well, kids, that's your decision. I certainly can sympathize. Arlene and I have been together for forty years, but there have been times . . ." And then the happy news dawned on him and tears came to his eyes and he had to blow his nose.

The happy news lit up the afternoon. An unseen child, in the house with them, a child sleeping inside his daughter. It was a quiet, happy dinner and a quiet afternoon washing dishes. Arlene took a nap, Clarence washed, Barbara Ann dried.

"I remember when I knew that your mother was expecting you. It was right around the beginning of July. A hot, beautiful day. I felt so good I walked downtown in my undershirt and bought a Panatela cigar and smoked it standing on the corner by Ralph's, and then I walked up to the co-op and bought four rockets and took them down to the swimming beach and stuck 'em in the gravel and shot 'em off, one, two, three, four, way out over the lake. Gosh, that was a day."

He could almost see those rockets bursting in air. Then Bill said, "Say, Dad, something's wrong with your fireplace." Clarence dashed out. Arlene was asleep on the sofa and starting to cough. Smoke filled the room. He opened the window and pitched burning logs out on the grass and heard a faraway siren, and in less time than it takes to talk about it, the old red truck came chugging up the driveway. "Thanks, boys," said Clarence. "No emergency—everything's under control."

They backed out and Bill decided he'd like to go for a long walk. Arlene went back to sleep. Clarence and Barbara Ann were in the kitchen when she felt the pain. "Mmhhhh," she said.

"What?"

"Nothing, a pain in my side. Mmmhhhh."

"Let's go," he said. "I'll get your coat."

"No, it's not that. It'll go away."

"Let's go. Now. I'll get the car out of the garage."

"Daddy, believe me. It's not that."

"Honey, there's no sense in taking a chance. Let's go."

And they went, but backing out of the driveway, he heard the fool-ishness of those words: "No sense in taking a chance." What else is having babies about if not taking a chance? They headed for the St. Cloud Hospital, but she felt better and the sun was setting and the pain was gone, so instead they drove to St. John's and back. What a fine chance to take. A lot of cars headed south from town, foreign cars going back to a life in the city that he did not understand: silent fathers, exhausted mothers, children sitting happily and politely with little headphones on their heads. We took a chance when we pro-duced these people, and it looks as if we'll have to wait a little longer to see how it comes out.

Myrrh is a sort of casserole, made from macaroni and hamburger or, as they say in the Mideast and Midwest, hammyrrh, thus the name. You bring it in a covered dish, thus the speculation that at least one of the Wise Men might have been one of our guys.

# 9

# The True Meaning of Christmas

It has been a quiet week in Lake Wobegon. The first Christmas visitor arrived on Monday, Sister Thorvaldson, Senator Thorvaldson's cousin. Sister was born near Lake Wobegon sixty-nine years ago and was named for a friend of the family who was a nun, although the Thorvaldsons weren't Catholic then or now, and she came up from Phoenix, where she's been living for a while. She never married—perhaps having the first name Sister discouraged her suitors—and she was lonely down there and missed the snow, so she came to stay with the Tollefsons. Byron Tollefson is her second nephew once removed on his mother's side. She said, "I hope it's no trouble. I could always stay at a motel." But of course it is trouble. It's just almost enough trouble that, without it, it wouldn't be Christmas. Besides, there's no room at the motel.

The Christmas decorations finally went up on Main Street on Tuesday—the angels, Wise Men, shepherds, and star, all made by old high school shop classes in their unit on plywood. Bud got them all up and hung the lights, a good day's work for an old guy. He wished those old shop students could've been around to help and maybe see why you don't need to use three-quarter-inch plywood—two sheets glued back to back. It was like hanging rocks. Bud has been campaigning for plastic decorations for years, but in Lake Wobegon they don't buy new until the old breaks, and these won't break, even when they're dropped from a great height. Bud knows—he's tried.

It's like Mr. Bauser at the post office, who hated his old Chevy but couldn't get rid of it because it still ran so good. Poor man. It was all rusted out on the sides, the floorboard on the driver's side was rusted away—he put in three-quarter-inch plywood—and he was sick of it for ten of the fifteen years he owned it, but this car, which was named Henry after his late father, would not die even after he quit doing maintenance. Lack of maintenance seemed to be good for it. It thrived on neglect. And something in Mr. Bauser's character, probably learned from his father, prevented him from disposing of this piece of junk because, on the coldest mornings, all he had to do was point at the ignition and it started up. He almost froze to death driving it on the coldest mornings, but Mr. Bauser was brought up to suffer discomfort cheerfully. So he drove it cheerfully even though it depressed the life out of him, until one day last December, the coldest December in memory, when a couple of men over lunch at the Chatterbox said, "Boy, the Chev of yours is sure a good starter, isn't it? What do you do to keep it running like that? I never had that sort of luck with a Chevy." Something in Mr. Bauser snapped, and he drove out west of town to the hill near the Halvorsons' and put her in neutral and got out and let her go and put that car out of his misery at the second telephone pole it hit. It was a happy man who walked a mile back to town. He's finished paying back the phone company now and he's got a new little car, Betty. It has its problems in cold weather, but when it does start, the heater works real good, and whether it starts or not, it has that new car smell, and that's really what he wanted. The feeling of newness, of starting over fresh.

It's a real Christmas feeling, the feeling of starting new, with fresh hope—it's how people who celebrate Christmas are supposed to feel, anyway. We know this and as Christmas builds up around us, we wait for some spark, some inspiration to touch our hearts, something more than nostalgia. Nostalgia is as easy as running a hot bath and getting in; you get out two pictures of yourself as a kiddo, and you're up to your waist in nostalgia. Nostalgia comes out of a faucet. We want to feel something else, something like wonder and joy, and if it doesn't come to us, we feel awful. Like going by yourself to the dance and discovering that you're the only one without a partner. Like going to a dinner and finding out after you get there that the invite said potluck. A through K bring a hotdish. L through R a salad. S through Z dessert. There you are, Mr. Blue, with nothing but a thin smile.

Pastor Ingqvist has been feeling blue—and that was what led to his surprising sermon at Lake Wobegon Lutheran last Sunday morning. His annual "True Meaning of Christmas" sermon. It's a tradition there and at Our Lady, too: both he and Father Emil set aside one Sunday before Christmas to throw some cold water on it. All over town, the presents are piling up and there's an avalanche of cookies in the kitchens, and it's time to talk about the needy and redemption and to say that Christmas can't be bought. It's a dirty job, but somebody's got to do it.

He was going to deliver this sermon on December 2, but he was too depressed. So instead he gave one on wonder and joy and the coming of the Child, though he was none too happy about his own children, who had been campaigning shamelessly for some pretty extravagant gifts, and none too happy with himself after he went out and bought them. These were the sorts of gifts you don't find at Skoglund's—he had to drive thirty miles to a huge discount store, four acres of merchandise under fluorescent lights that are designed to drive people quietly berserk, and all around him he saw people quietly going over the edge, losing the powers of reason, filling shopping carts with very attractively packaged junk, people who were driven by some inner urge like sheep, mumbling to themselves, "No payments till Jaaaaaanuary." Children in a fever, pleading, whining. Parents dazed, bewildered, pleading, threatening. Salesclerks who looked like they were in the eighth round, with a bad headache, looking for a place to fall. Pastor Ingqvist got in and out as fast as he could, but he spent half an hour in line at the checkout counter. Half an hour of exposure to some deadly invisible rays, and a long drive home to wonder, *Why have I bought my children a video game called* Annihilation *for Christmas? Because they asked for it? Who's in charge around here? Who's running Christmas this year?*

It was Friday night, and Saturday he wrote the sermon, and Sunday he gave it and said that the true meaning of Christmas is thus-and-so and if Christmas doesn't serve that purpose, then we ought to throw it away even if it's still running. That was the beginning, the middle, and the conclusion of his sermon.

He stood up under the Advent candles behind a pulpit decorated with red and green paper chains made by a Sunday school in a sanctuary that smelled of pine boughs, and he read this sobering sermon in a very definite tone of voice—if our hearts aren't right, then let's get rid of Christmas and throw it out, all of it—until he got to the end of page one and paused before he launched into the next paragraph and he heard a child crying and looked up and there down in the fourth row was his little boy sitting next to Mrs. Ingqvist looking up at him with tears running down his cheeks. His mouth was open, his lower lip was trembling, and his breath came in gasps—"Oh no, oh no, Daddy, I'll be good, I promise."

It's not easy being a minister and preaching to your own family— sometimes it gives a Lutheran pastor real respect for the rule of celibacy over across town. Preach on forgiveness and forbearance to a congregation that includes one woman with whom you've had some arguments you'd rather not remember, including one that isn't over yet.

It wasn't easy to put his sermon aside and wing it for ten minutes, but he did. It wasn't the best sermon he ever gave, but then, the church-goers of Lake Wobegon don't go in for comparison shopping, and he used up some ideas he was going to use in his sermon for next Sunday, but he had a week to think about that, so he just let it fly.

He talked about the Wise Men who traveled far from the east following the star to Bethlehem. They are not prominent figures in the Christmas story, but of all the characters, they're the only ones who probably weren't Jewish but rather Gentile—and therefore, conceivably, Lutheran. We think they might have been Lutheran because they brought gifts: gold, frankincense, and myrrh. Myrrh is a sort of casserole, made from macaroni and hamburger or, as they say in the Mideast and Midwest, hammyrrh, thus the name. You bring it in a covered dish, thus the speculation that at least one of the Wise Men might have been one of our guys. Maybe he was going to stop at the department store and get something expensive like gold or frankincense, but his wife, a Wise Woman, said, "Here, take this myrrh. They'll be hungry. And make sure you bring back the dish."

They followed a star to the stable, which, for Wise Men, is not particularly smart when you stop and think about it, because a star is in the sky and the sense of direction you get from it is pretty general, and which stable the star is over depends a lot on where you are standing—so they were navigating by faith. They made a long trip based on less hard information than a person might like to have, but they came through to that first and perfect Christmas. And so may we. It's an adventure, maybe more for us than for them because we have so many distractions and there is so much artificial light and reflected light that it's hard to see stars in the sky. But certainly it is possible to find the way to Christmas, and that was his revised sermon on Sunday.

And then church was over and they all marched out into the snow and home for pot roast. Sometimes when you walk out that door after church, you are inspired and expect things to look different—expect to walk out and be in the New Jerusalem—and it's a disappointment to see it's still Lake Wobegon. A vacant lot across the street, dogs running around, the Dieners' house unpainted and two broken-down cars in the backyard, and the back door of the Sidetrack Tap—the scene of so much illness and unhappiness over the years. But even here there is a star to follow, and we may come through.

# 10

# "Johnny Johnson's Wedding": The Sons of Knute Christmas Song

Oh, we had a lovely party in Lake Wobegon last night;
Everyone was there with their faces shining bright.
We don't all like each other and yet we reunite
At the Sons of Knute Christmas dance and dinner.

Oh, the glitter and the candles and the gifts at every place;
It almost brought a smile to an old Norwegian's face.
We went around and we shook hands,
Though of course we don't embrace,
Except sometimes we'll sort of hug you sideways.

There was Clarence Peterson and Hjalmar Peterson
And Gladys Peterson and Lois Peterson
And Carl Peterson and Laura Peterson
and Pete Peterson—he was there too.

There was knackebrod and herring and old Norwegian cheese
Strong enough to bring a bachelor farmer to his knees
And an old Icelandic aquavit that tastes like antifreeze;
You have a glass and you cannot feel your tonsils.

I sat next to Hjalmar Peterson, now there's a tough old bird.
We sat and chewed our lutefisk and we didn't say a word,
'Cause everything we have to say we've already heard.
So what's the use of pointless conversation?

There was Clarence Larson and Hjalmar Larson
And Gladys Larson and Lois Larson
And Carl Larson and Judy Larson
And Lars Larson—he was there too.

We had three quarts of whiskey and a couple kegs of beer,
And everyone drank faster as we saw it disappear.
Then Svendson got out the aquavit and everybody cheered,
And we drank a toast to the king and queen of Norway.

And for Lutherans, don't you know, it was a festive atmosphere.
And when I dropped my trousers, boy,
They'll be talking about that all year
At the Sons of Knute Christmas dance and dinner.

There was Clarence Nilssen and Hjalmar Nilssen
And Gladys Nilssen and Lois Nilssen
And Ray Nilssen and Jenny Nilssen
And Nils Nilssen—he was there too.

I raised my hands for silence and then I told a joke;
It was a pretty raw one, not meant for decent folk.
And Pastor Jonsson laughed so hard
I thought he'd have a stroke,
And he blew some tapioca out his nostrils.

Well, everyone was scandalized by this debauchery
And they gossiped and they shook their heads so regretfully,
By God they had a wonderful night, and it was thanks to me
At the Sons of Knute Christmas dance and dinner.

There was Clarence Oleson and Hjalmar Oleson
And Gladys Oleson and Lois Oleson
And Carl Oleson and Carolyn Oleson
And Ole Oleson—he was there too.

And then we moved the tables and let the fun begin;
Evelyn played piano and Lester the violin.
Larry blew on the saxophone,
And oh, you could smell the gin
As they struck up the "Beer Barrel Polka."

I got up from the table the moment I heard the band;
I danced with all the teenage girls, I held 'em by the hand.
There's nothing warms an old man's heart
Like a sweet young woman can
At the Sons of Knute Christmas dance and dinner.

There was Christina Larson and Christina Svendson
And Christina Peterson and Christina Oleson
And Christina Anderson and Christina Johnson
And then my wife said, "That's enough for you."

Then at two o'clock in the morning
We finally swept all the trash away
And put on our overcoats and said a last adieu.

We said good-bye in the hallway
And said good-bye on the stairs;
We said good-bye on the sidewalk in the cold December air.
Then we leaned against the cars and said good-bye out there.
Boy, it was the best darn party ever.

And the next day when we woke up, we were sick in bed;
Our stomachs were kind of rocky
And there was hammering in our head.
But that evening we felt better and we sat up and said,
"Boy, that was a heck of a Christmas party."

[
*Christmas can't make you happy.*
*Little things make you happy, like a nice rice pudding.*
*Or ice fishing.*
]

# Ice Fishing

I t's been cold this week, and the lake has frozen up almost a foot thick, and it froze with no wind and no snow, so it's perfectly clear smooth ice. When that immense full moon rose through the trees, people skated across the lake in the bright moonlight, trailing moon shadows and looking down and gazing at the bottom, watching the sunfish and crappies and walleyes down there feeding in the moonlight.

The fish houses have been hauled out onto the ice, and a whole little community established, with the houses lined up along streets and avenues marked on the ice with pylons, the streets numbered one through ten, the avenues alphabetical: Aldrich, Bryant, Colfax, Dupont, Emerson, Fremont, Girard, Humboldt, Irving, James, Knox, Logan, Morgan, Newton, Oliver, Penn, Queen, Russell, Sheridan, and Tip Up. These are German and Scandinavian folks in Lake Wobegon, and even though it's a frozen lake, they like to have some order to it. You can't just let people plop down wherever they want to.

Ice fishing is a form of monasticism, and this year some of the monks were complaining about the old lady making them take a cell phone out to the fish house so they could call her up and let her know when they'd be in for supper. The fish house is a place where you go to forget about time. You get in your car and drive out on the ice, and when you get to your shack, you have escaped from work and your family and clocks and schedules and forms and reports and arrived at the place of sanity.

A vast expanse of ice and such silence, such grandeur.

You open your shack and light a fire in the stove and put the coffeepot on to boil, and you put a minnow on a hook and drop it into the hole and reach for the whiskey bottle, which you keep for medicinal purposes to kill off viruses and to ward off the chill and to flavor your coffee, and you have arrived at a point of serenity and peace that tycoons and movie stars could only envy, and then your phone rings. No phone has rung in this shack in its entire history. You let it ring a few times so they get the idea, and then you pick it up. It's your beloved wife. She says, "Do you have any idea at all when you might be home?" And you feel time tap you on the shoulder. You feel the fence go up. A lid is put on the day. A line is tied to your ankle.

So now even ice fishing, in all its sanity and silence, has been blighted by the curse of this century, which is communications. Never before have we learned so much we didn't need to know from people we don't like and can't get rid of in media that has only one purpose, to sell, sell, sell, and which has been steadily encroaching and circling and crowding out whatever peace and quiet is left in the cosmos and stirring up restlessness and envy and greed and impatience.

Some ice fishermen this year have portable houses, like tents, so if the fish aren't hitting one place they can try another, but they are younger guys, and the older guys in the fish houses disapprove of this. Lake Wobegon is not a nomadic culture; we believe in staying put and letting success come to you. That's our philosophy. We are not an impatient people chasing after the rainbow. Impatience is disastrous—it breaks up perfectly good marriages, it is rough on kids, it is confusing to dogs and other animals, it destroys careers, and it results in people catching less fish than if they'd just stayed put.

Ralph's Pretty Good Grocery was crowded yesterday morning with ambitious people buying pimientos and whole cashews and canned oysters and exotic cheeses, like Gorgonzola and Camembert, and odd spices and exotic mushrooms, and you could tell they'd gotten hold of a magazine article with beautiful color photos of dishes. They were throwing caution to the wind and putting the candied yams and turkey aside in favor of gourmet cuisine, and you knew that some of these cuisine adventures were going to end in heartbreak, in smoke-filled kitchens with frazzled cooks weeping into their aprons and coming unhinged.

Lake Wobegon Lutheran Church held a 5:30 service on Christmas Eve that was packed with people, many of them unfamiliar faces, strays, the unchurched, and the church smelled of pine boughs and candles and the children's choir processed up the aisle singing, "A child is born in Bethlehem . . . Bethlehem . . . that gladdens all Jerusalem. Alleluia. Alleluia," and you bow your head and weep. That is the heart of Christmas right there—it's all anyone would need—but when Pastor Ingqvist stepped into the pulpit, all the strangers, the unchurched, looked to him as if he would bring magic, some word to transform them, and the sermon would change their lives. But it was only him, Friendly Dave; it wasn't St. Augustine, as the regulars know very well. The strangers felt let down by a sermon that was brief and mentioned the Nativity, though there was quite a bit about the Norwegian Christmas elf, the nisse, and it wasn't easy to follow, and it was far from being a transforming moment, and even with the beautiful conclusion to the service—everyone holding a little white candle with a paper "collar" for the singing of "Silent Night"—you could tell that people felt let down. Disappointed by Christmas, because we're not as joyful as we think we ought to be.

Christmas is a holy day that the early church fathers invented because they were in competition with the Roman religion. One thing Christianity lacked was a big feast, and the Romans had one toward the end of December, Saturnalia, so the Christians established Christmas, sort of like one chain putting up a store right near its competitor. It doesn't have so much to do with Jesus as it does with business, and it's been a big hit: the number of people celebrating Saturnalia and offering sacrifices to the gods has really diminished.

The Puritans weren't into Christmas, knowing how shaky it was theologically, and the holiday was brought to America by the Dutch. It was in New York that Christmas became American with the invention of Santa Claus. It was in 1820 that Clement Clark Moore, living down in Chelsea, which was uptown then, coming home in his sleigh with the Christmas turkey, got the idea to write a poem for his children, "A Visit from St. Nicholas," which a friend of his copied down and sent to a newspaper in Troy, New York, which published it without attribution. Mr. Moore was a professor of Hebrew and Greek at the seminary down on Ninth Avenue and Twentieth Street, and he had no wish to go down in history as the author of light verse, though of course he did.

His poem gave us a picture of Santa Claus that was new and American. The Dutch version was less jolly: Sinterklaas came on Christmas and put cinders in the stockings of bad children. Professor Moore took out the judicial element and made him a sort of jolly uncle who brings you whatever you want no matter what. And the cartoonist Thomas Nast drew the picture of him as a rotund fellow with rosy cheeks and a big grin.

The Norwegians had never seen him as jolly either. They believed in the Christmas elf, the nisse, who was mischievous if not actually malicious and who came around on Christmas Eve. You had to leave him a gift of rice pudding, because it was he who would decide whether you had good luck or not so good. The nisse didn't bring gifts; he got them. He tasted your rice pudding, and if it wasn't creamy enough or if it was too creamy or if there weren't enough almonds in it, he wrinkled up his face and the next week you had a terrible earache, and the week after that a tree fell on your garage, and then your dad went in for prostate surgery. You had to learn to make rice pudding the way the nisse liked it. Otherwise, your life would be rotten. And even if you made great rice pudding, sometimes the nisse out of pure meanness would make your toilets back up and get the IRS to call you in for an audit, and you'd get that straightened out and then the doorbell would ring and you'd open the door to find Mike Wallace and a cameraman filming. The stock would go down. Your newsboy would sue you because he tripped over the hose. You'd get your water tested; it's got lead in it. One thing after another. All because of the pudding.

Some of us feel that this is truer to life than the idea of a fat man coming down the chimney and giving you all of your heart's desires. It's no wonder Clement Moore didn't want his name put on his poem— he was embarrassed by it. He was a theologian; he knew he had created a commercial legend that would help sell things and that would

cause disappointment, envy, impatience. What made him do it? It was
a nisse who wrote the poem, out of sheer meanness.

Christmas can't make you happy. Little things make you happy, like
a nice rice pudding. Or ice fishing.

Mr. Berge went out to his ice house on Christmas Eve, he said just to
check on things and he'd be right back, but his wife knows him after all
these years—she knows what "check on things" means and the actual
time frame involved in "coming right back"—and she made him take a
cell phone out there. And first he pretended not to hear her, and then
he got a roll of cellophane—"Is this what you meant?"

"No," she said, "you're seventy-six years old, and I worry about you
going out there all alone. Take the cell phone with you."

He drove out onto the ice. The big moon in the sky. All was still,
all was light. He lit the stove, made the coffee, put the whiskey in the
coffee, and stood outside and sipped it and looked toward the lights of
town, the streetlights and the pale lighted windows and in every house,
like a jewel, that cluster of red and green and blue of the Christmas
tree. The coffee was so good, with the whiskey, in the cold. He walked
into the fish house and took the cell phone out of his jacket pocket
and dropped it into the hole in the ice, like dropping a clothespin into
a milk bottle, and there was a lovely splosh and it disappeared, and he
felt a little burst of happiness, pure joy.

## 12

# The Sons of Knute March

Sons of Knute we are, sons of the prairie,
With our heads held high in January,
Hauling our carcass around in big parkas,
Wearing boots the size of tree stumps.

Now the temperature's fourteen below zero,
And according to the Weather Bureau
The wind chill is minus one hundred, your sinus
Is frozen, and your poor brass monkey.

There is ice in your hair and ice on your eyeballs,
Ice in your bed and ice on your Bibles.
Your auto's ignition is out of commission;
You turn the key, it clicks and whimpers.

We don't talk about art or beauty or wisdom.
Art is our plumber—we called him, we missed him.
The toilet's not flushin', and so the discussion
Is all about when Art might get here.

And when March comes round and the snowbanks are dirty
And a cold rain falls and sunset's five thirty,
We are heroic, silent and stoic.
We hunker down and read trash novels.

And spring finally comes, but then the paper'll
Say that more snow's forecast the end of April.
We rise up like eagles and jump in our vehicles
    And drive off to the mall and buy stuff.

    Oh, we don't care, we wear a smile;
    We are folks who believe in denial.
    We can't afford a trip down to Florida,
    So we're doing just fine, thank you.

*We don't come from a siesta culture.
It's a work-for-the-night-is-coming culture.*

# 13

# Ministers' Retreat

It has been a quiet week in Lake Wobegon. It's been cold here, and very pretty with fresh snow on the ground and people's outdoor Christmas lights still up, and the pace of things slows down when the wind chill is minus thirty-five. People move deliberately from house to car and car to Chatterbox Café. Walking outside is like swimming underwater: you know you cannot last long in that medium, but it's only so fast you can go in it, too.

So the Ingqvists skipped some of the sessions to enjoy a few hours together lying on chaise lounges at poolside and feeling the sun on their skin and smelling the flowers and enjoying a drink whose purpose is to stimulate an afternoon nap, always a problem for a Lutheran. Ours is not a siesta culture. It's a work-for-the-night-is-coming culture.

They reclined by the pool as people do on vacation, and they talked about their friends and neighbors back home in a frank way that wouldn't be possible at home with children within earshot.

They speculated about the anonymous donor who has provided this vacation the past three years. An old parishioner, they figure. One who slid away from the church and made some money and feels guilty about it, and good for him. What would we do without guilt? A guilty conscience is better than no conscience at all.

All around them, other Lutherans playing hooky from pastoral camp, feeling guilty about not being the people God wants them to be, lay in God's sunshine, under God's palm trees, and drank beverages created from God's lemons and oranges, and God's potatoes, and felt sleepy.

The Ingqvists talked about what people back home were probably doing at that moment. How strange to think that even then, as they lay under the sun, slathered with heavy-duty sun cream, back home people were walking into the wind, heads bowed, shuffling over the ice, bundled up like members of another race. And then a man in white shorts bent over them and they looked up and said, yes, they would like a refill; it's very tasty, thank you.

In the Chatterbox Café, they were talking about the impeachment proceedings in the Senate, though it's hard for people in my hometown, who live in the real world, to get a handle on unreality. There have been times, goodness knows, when Congress has been out of touch, but the whole impeachment saga is a long trip down the rabbit hole. Up above ground, the country goes along with its business, and down the hole where Congress lives, the Confederacy rises again, the Republican South rides to overthrow the presidency, and it's hard to have a rational opinion about it except to wish it would end as soon as possible, and then that the long chain of sorry characters who promulgated this ordeal find work in some other field such as pest control and start with themselves.

The impeachment proceedings reminded some of the patrons of when they were boys and would get cherry bombs and use them to blow up cow pies. You'd find the right cow pie, with enough of a crust to hold the wick upright, but viscous enough so it would fly, and you'd light the wick and run so you'd be beyond the perimeter of impact. You'd stop to watch, and sometimes you'd miscalculate and the bomb went off and you'd see flying dung shrapnel heading your way and duck and get some in your hair and a big gob in your ear—that's what the impeachment gang is up to. They've put a bomb in a very soft cow pie, and they are not as swift afoot as they think they are.

Sometimes when you make a dash for it in a pasture, you step into a cow pie that moments before you decided was too soft to hold the charge. This may happen as well.

When it gets bitterly cold in Lake Wobegon, it seems more crowded because people here are twice as big with their big down parkas on, and their boots, and in Ralph's Pretty Good Grocery, two people can hardly pass in the aisle. And people going into church—it's like a parade of dirigibles. But last Sunday, one dirigible was bigger than all the others, and that was the substitute pastor at Lake Wobegon Lutheran, Pastor Sorenson.

He flew up from Minneapolis Saturday night in his little Beech-craft, equipped with skis, and landed by prior arrangement in Roger Hedlund's cornfield, and Roger and Cindy took him in for the night. He was six-feet-five and weighed about 320, bald, with a fringe of blond hair, and solidly built, and Roger was too polite to ask, but Pastor Sorenson did remind Roger of somebody he had seen once. They sat and ate meat loaf and twice-baked potatoes and talked about the weather, and it wasn't until after dinner that Cindy—to whom Roger had mentioned the resemblance when they cleared the table and rinsed the plates—brought out the apple pie and ice cream and looked at the visitor and said, "You look an awful lot like someone we saw on TV once—we don't watch TV much, and we just happened to be changing channels, and we came on a professional wrestling bout, and one of the wrestlers was being interviewed and—"

And Pastor Sorenson nodded. "That was me," he said. "Before I got the call."

He was a football player at Augustana and wasn't sure what to do after school. He was thinking about seminary but felt he wasn't ready, and he went to work as a trainer at a gym in Minneapolis, and wres-tlers came there to work out, and that's how he got into the field. It was like a fraternity; they were all brothers—the heroes and villains, the faces and the heels—and it was a lot harder than it looked, two guys moving around a ring, playing out the script, doing the piledriv-ers and the flying mules, bouncing off the ropes, doing the bumps, pacing the action, creating the heat, getting the crowd going, which was the whole point of it. He had wrestled under several names.

He started out as a hero, Blind Boy Barnes, and wore dark glasses and had a guide dog named Klaus, who was beautifully trained and part of the act. When the villain got Blind Boy down using the usual dirty tricks, a nostril hold or an ankle stomp or the use of foreign sub-stances, and Blind Boy lay helpless as the villain applied the deadly spinal tap hold and the dog stood in the corner, front paws on the top rope, agitated, then Blind Boy would raise his left leg, and that was the signal. Klaus would leap into the ring and go for the villain's throat, the hapless referee would wave his hands, bewildered, and Blind Boy would rise up in rage and apply the pin.

Then he became a heel. He put on a turban and became the Ayatollah Khomeanie, and then he had a monocle and a riding whip and was Das Kapitan Werner von Wehrmacht, and then he became the masked wrestler the Hedlunds had seen—the Messenger of Death.

He came into the ring wearing a black hangman's mask, his body smeared with gore, carrying the bloody head of a dead woman in his right hand, viscera hanging from it, and once the match began, the Messenger circled the ring slowly, slowly, slowly, and got into a clinch. The opponent put a few moves on him and the Messenger got whacked around for a while, and then suddenly he went berserk and grabbed some two-by-fours, a lead pipe, a sledgehammer, a plumber's wrench, and there followed fifteen minutes of utterly wacko nonstop barbaric violence and unspeakable atrocities. The ring was dripping blood and the Messenger pulled out a Zippo and lit the ropes and they burst into flame; the whole ring was surrounded by fire, the opponent was pounded to a pulp, and the audience stood in horror and admiration, drunk on forty-ounce cups of beer, and cheered as the Messenger raged up the aisle waving his hammer and disappeared into the dressing room.

He did that for three years and saved up money to put himself through seminary.

Cindy said, "Didn't you—I mean, as a Lutheran—didn't you—you know, did it seem—odd?"

The Messenger of Death looked down at his pie and said, "I looked on it as a work of atonement," he said. "It's hard to explain."

And then as Lutherans always do when they come to a hard place in the conversation, they changed the subject and talked about his airplane.

Cindy didn't say a word to anybody about Pastor Sorenson's history except her sister in Minneapolis, and somehow from that one leak the news got around, and on Sunday morning the church was packed with people. They watched the gigantic man in the black robe come up the aisle during the opening hymn and do the confession of sins and the announcements and lead the prayers and read the Gospel and give the sermon, and it was not a bad sermon. Sort of dry. Rather short. They were expecting something more passionate from the Messenger of

Death, but he looked not well at all, as if the steroids had gone sour on him. He looked like a small man in a large body, an act of puppetry.

And then at the end of the service, he said an odd thing. He said, "I have to fly home this afternoon, but if there is anyone here who requires pastoral care, I'll be in the church office for an hour after the conclusion of the service."

Well, people filed out. Nobody went to the office. You don't like to march up there in front of everyone. On the other hand, wouldn't it be impolite to let the man sit there alone for an hour and feel that people were avoiding him because of his background in the ring?

People went home, and half an hour later a car pulled up in the parking lot and Clint Bunsen got out with a package and went into the church. A lot of people saw this out their windows.

Clint walked in the office as the Messenger of Death was putting on his big leather coat. Clint explained that in the package was a box containing the ashes of his late brother-in-law, Bob, his wife's brother, who had died at the age of fifty-eight, a Lutheran who'd gone into the lucrative office park development business and made a pile and also lost his faith, and he'd specified cremation and hadn't wanted a funeral, so they didn't have one, but Irene would feel so much better if Pastor Sorenson would scatter the ashes over the old family farm a few miles south of town and say a prayer—it was on his way home—and the pastor agreed and took the box, and the plane took off from the pasture, and he flew south and located the farm, the windmill, the red barn, and circled back around and banked steeply. He had it all worked out how he was going to do this, and he opened the window and threw out the remains, and the blast from the wind blew the ashes back in and covered the interior of the plane and the Messenger of Death's coat and his hair and face; he was all gray when he landed back at the Hedlunds' pasture.

Cindy got a vacuum and put a fresh bag in it out of respect for the deceased, and his ashes were collected, and Roger agreed that he would take the bag to the Olson farm. The plane took off again, and as it disappeared, heading south, Roger realized that he had the minister's check in his pocket. He had forgotten. And he didn't even have the minister's address. They would have to wait for the Messenger of Death to ask for payment, and what if he didn't? Then they would be cheating death, and what sort of trouble might a person get in for that?

*Scripture says, "Be still and know that I am God."*
*This is not the organist's philosophy. Organists despise stillness.*
*They're sitting there with the organ equivalent of a 300 hp Ferrari*
*and they want to put the pedal to the metal and make that baby fly.*

# 14

# Church Organist

It has been a quiet week in Lake Wobegon. It's been very cold, and for people who are sort of drifting along in life, waiting for their ship to come in, it's sort of a wake-up call. Winter is the moral equivalent of war. And the harbor is frozen shut. No ships this week. But there is your walk to shovel.

Tibby Marklund, the organist at Lake Wobegon Lutheran, has taken time off to go tend to her father-in-law who is dying in Duluth. She sits with him in hospice care and holds his hand as he looks out his window, out across Lake Superior and the solid ice mass there. He's been in hospice for three weeks and has been improving. Was near death when he arrived, or seemed to be, and then they took him off the antibiotics and he bounced back, and now is getting up and walking around. Tibby thinks he is postponing. Maybe waiting for the ground to warm up. He doesn't talk about death at all. Or God. He talks about his car. He wants her to go start it. It needs to run every day in this cold weather; otherwise it won't start. Surely a good maxim for all of us.

She sits by his bed reading the handbook on dying that the hospice nurse has given her. It is full of sentences like "Spirituality carries a deep and personal meaning unique to each of us and our beliefs and values and personal philosophy." It advises you to forgive the dying person, to express your love and your gratitude, and to say good-bye. She thinks that if she ever said "I love you" to this old Swede, it would kill him. It almost killed him when she married into the family. She's

Jewish and from the east and married her phlegmatic Swede because she loved him and saw that he was more than he appeared to be, and she also saw that life with him would be easier than if she married somebody dashing and romantic and brilliant. A brief shining moment of wisdom in her confused youth, and she is so grateful for it. A little wisdom now and then is enough for anybody, if your timing is right. It has been an easy marriage. Good father, sweet husband, does guy jobs like disposing of deceased animals and removing bats from the fireplace and also cooks now and then, and he is much the same from week to week. You don't go to bed with Mark Twain and wake up with the Marquis de Sade.

And she thinks that death itself is easy. What is so dreadful in contemplation, what gives us fits all our lives, turns out to be, in most cases, when you come up to it, fairly simple and ordinary and modest and decent. The body slowly shuts down, consciousness diminishes, the mind lets go. Except with this old Swede in Duluth. The problem is that death is too easy and he's always preferred the hard tasks. So he's clinging to life. For the challenge of it.

The substitute organist who showed up last Sunday made almost all the Lutherans wish that Tibby's father-in-law would die immediately. Of course, when you shop for a substitute organist, you're looking at damaged goods, and you know it, and with organists, less is more. Same with ministers. Gradually the worship committee is getting Pastor Ingqvist down to fifteen and twelve minutes, and a few Sundays he's managed to get down to ten. The five-minute homily remains a distant dream, but it is attainable. It's not hard to do. You just write your usual six-page sermon and throw away the first page and all the attempts to be ingratiating or conversational or folksy, and you get a couple of sentences from the bottom of the second page and a paragraph or two from page three, and you edit page four down to about fifty words, and you throw away five and six. And there you are. It's not hard; what's hard is getting up the will to do it.

Tibby Marklund is an ideal organist. She's a violinist by training, had a little piano, taught herself to play the organ, can't play very well and is aware of it. That's the best organist you could hope for. A one-handed organist would be good, too. A one-handed legless organist even better. The organ is the enemy of worship, as most Christians know. Scripture says, "Be still and know that I am God." This is not the organist's philosophy. Organists despise stillness. They're sitting there with the organ equivalent of a 300 hp Ferrari and they want to put the pedal to the metal and make that baby fly. This dude came up from the Cities early Sunday morning—he'd sent up an anthem and a motet for the offertory, sent them up for the choir to rehearse Tuesday night, and they couldn't make head nor tail of it—the motet was in French, for crying out loud, and the anthem was a piece of fifteenth-century plainsong with odd little square notes—so instead they practiced "Praise to the Lord, the Almighty, the King of Creation" for the anthem and "What a Friend We Have in Jesus" for the offertory.

He arrived Sunday morning, this pale, thin man with colorless hair and no chin and wire-rimmed glasses, got out of his big boat of a car with an armload of music, came trudging into church, looked at the organ with barely disguised contempt, then looked at what the choir had prepared with barely disguised contempt, and heaved a big sigh and settled in to endure the humiliation of subjecting his vast talent to this throng of Philistines. He warmed up for half an hour, with five or six incredibly virtuosic pieces, all of which he knew by heart—it was like the artillery barrage before the invasion, to stun them into submission. For the prelude he chose a big heroic French piece that showed off his footwork. People arriving in church thinking they were coming to see God found themselves at an organ concert, and the music was not about contrition or humility. It was about triumph. Mastery. Sadism. Leather whips. Barbed wire.

The opening hymn was a hymn nobody had ever sung before in their lives. The Lutheran Book of Worship was, of course, put together by a committee, and there are hymns there that you know were included as a sop to the closet Anglicans on the committee, those weird hymns that reflected the mood of a community of monks living on a rocky island off Wales in the fifteenth century. The opening hymn was a sort of musical hair shirt, something in a minor key with weird intervals, and it sounded like there should have been bagpipes, and if you weren't celibate and didn't have forty years in which to devote your-self to it, it was basically unsingable, so the first verse was the most pitiful sound that can come out of a congregation. It sounded like a fishing village keening for its dead. There were eight verses. He meant the choir to sing all of them. A sort of torture. And he played louder and louder, evidently thinking this would inspire them, but it had the opposite effect. Like most organ playing, it made you lose your inter-est in music; it made you sit up resolute and brave and try to think back to a very happy time in your life and meditate on that, as you do in the dentist's chair. During the sixth verse, Cindy Hedlund in the alto section leaned over and said to Marilyn Hedlund, "He's not the organist; he's the Enforcer."

Cindy has sung in choir since she was little. She played in school orchestra. She knows the rules. You are polite, you come on time, you pay attention, you do your best, you do what the conductor says no matter how ridiculous. If the conductor says, "I want this to be very dry but with a lot of vibrato," you do it. "I want this very quiet but very big." You do it. You don't talk back. You don't criticize your col-leagues. You're a musician, not a critic. You don't glare at somebody who just sang a quarter step flat. You don't badmouth people, unless to your husband maybe or your sister or your best friend. And if the conductor is a jerk, you don't react; you keep a stone face. But after the offertory Cindy lost her cool. He had decided that "What a Friend We Have in Jesus" was simply something he could not be personally associated with, a popular hymn, a hymn that these peasants knew practically by heart. No, he waved off the choir and instead played the offertory, some medieval-sounding thing with trumpets and sack-buts in it and dukes and the Marquis de Sade and armor clanking, and when it was done, Cindy Hedlund got up and walked down to the organist and leaned down and whispered a word in his ear. One simple English word for a part of the anatomy that each of us has, men and women, young and old, rich and poor. And she walked out of the church and got in her car and drove home.

Roger was there. He hadn't gone to church. She was glad he hadn't. He's been under enough stress. He's trying to decide whether to get out of farming and retire at the age of fifty-eight, which something in him really wants to do, but on the other hand he doesn't want to give up the cause. Farmers are some of the most idealistic people you'd ever hope to meet. Working outdoors can have that effect on people. And the family farm is a hopeless cause. Like the Northwest Passage or the gold fields of northern Minnesota or live radio, and for him it is especially hopeless because his two daughters have no interest in farming nor any interest in men who might be interested in farming, and his wife has no interest either, so unless he wants to start a new family, this farm is a dead end.

He was in the kitchen, just finishing up replacing a pane of glass in the window over the sink. He was surprised to see her. He thought he had another half hour to get the job done so she wouldn't ever have to know about it. What happened was, they redid the kitchen, thinking they'd sell the farm, so they wanted to fix up the house—which he, being Norwegian, wouldn't have done if they were going to stay in it. So to improve the value, he put in a breakfast nook and a cooking island with a butcher block top and a pot rack overhead, and it's hung so that Cindy can reach it, but that means the pots are where Roger tends to bump his head on them, and this morning he banged his head on a skillet and lost his temper and grabbed the thing and threw it and it busted the window.

He thought she'd be mad, but after you've just escaped from the Lord of Darkness at the organ keyboard, nothing that happens afterward is that bad. She got down the skillet and put it on the stove.

"What are you doing?"

"Going to make dinner."

"In that?"

"In that."

She put a pot of water on to boil and put about three tablespoons of butter in the skillet and melted that, and then she chopped up some onion, minced it, and tossed that in the butter and cooked it until it was glassy, and then she dumped in a can of diced tomatoes and added salt and pepper and let it simmer.

It's nothing that anybody in Lake Wobegon could ever bring themselves to say out loud, because it sounds like bragging, and it's bad luck to brag, and the moment you say it, you break your mother's back and

a hailstorm starts moving your way and your pigs lie down in the pen
with their feet in the air and somewhere in the Cities your daughter
goes out the door with an older married man. It's bad luck, but nonetheless she was thinking it: there does come a point in life where a great
deal that used to be worrisome simply becomes easier. It's surprising
how easy life can get. I associate this with winter, when the weather
gets cold and sometimes ferocious, and life inside becomes simpler
and lovelier. A man and woman look at each other across the breakfast table and realize it's been a long time since they've had bad feelings about each other, these two who've gone through rough patches
when big arguments could come up suddenly out of nowhere that left
them emotionally drained and sorrowful for days, and now it feels as
if they've turned a corner and found something easy, a simple pleasure
in each other, in their domestic arrangements, in their mutual life, in
lying in bed and rubbing her back, in walking into the bathroom and
she turns naked and beautiful and looks at you without alarm. It's so
easy when it's easy. You come to this time unaware of it, and gradually
it dawns on you that you don't covet anything anymore, you're not
ambitious for yourself anymore, you enjoy the success of other people
and are happy for them, and you see so often how unable they are to
be happy about their own success, but that's not your problem. You've
come to this sweet time in life.

She put the spaghetti in the boiling water. She hummed the offertory: "What a friend we have in Jesus, all our sins and griefs to bear. . . ."
It's Grandma's Spaghetti. A wonderful dish for people who've had too
much cuisine and been eating in restaurants where the waiter recites
the recipe of each special dish, who've tried too hard to make their
own noodles and do the sauce from the recipe that starts out, "Two
days before, marinade the chopped chicken livers in a half cup of salt-
free soy sauce—I prefer the kind from the northern islands, which is
available in most Asian food specialty stores." For people who've been
trying too hard, Grandma's Spaghetti is a great treat. The chopped
tomatoes simmer in the chopped onion and butter—you can add gar-
lic, if you like, or not. Or basil. Or not. And the spaghetti cooks. And
you take the spaghetti out of the water and put it in the sauce and
moosh it around and serve it up with grated Parmesan on top and it's

good. And easy. "Oh, what peace we often forfeit, oh, what needless pain we bear. . . . In His arms He'll take and shield you; you will find a solace there."

[ *They still work from that 4-3-2 formation,*
*even as other ushers have gone to a zone,*
*and their secret still is quickness and anticipation.* ]

# 15

# The Herdsmen

It has been a quiet week in Lake Wobegon. It was colder this
week but not cold enough, and the skating and the ice fishing are
over, which is a big disappointment. It's a dull, depressing time
of year anyway. Lately the sky has been bright pink in the early morning, so beautiful, and then the sun comes up and you see what's around
you—snow half melted, crusty, your backyard looking like bison have
camped there, garbage strewn by the dogs.

Valentine's Day is Tuesday, and what does that mean? Chocolate,
which we don't need, or flowers—we hate to think of how much you
paid for them. Flowers from Mexico—you shouldn't have done it.

The Herdsmen were winners in the Church Ushers Competition
Thursday night in Houston, Texas. They beat out a Baptist usher team, a
Methodist, and were first runners-up to a Jewish team called Parkyercar-
cass. The Herdsmen came home Friday with the first-runner-up trophy,
and it was nothing to people. Nothing. A national award. That's how
Lake Wobegon can be in February. Dark and discouraging. The Herdsmen used to have that great front four of Don, John, Louie, and Boomer
back in the seventies. And Boomer, he was an usher's usher. The man
worked a sanctuary on Sunday morning like you wouldn't believe. With
Boomer you didn't have people filling up the back rows first—he moved
'em right down front. Boomer was a big man, and he got his nickname
from his voice, which would strip wallpaper. He'd been a basketball coach
and did some auctioneering and raised six kids, and no matter where
they were, they could hear Boomer when he called them for supper.

As head usher, Boomer pretty much ran things in the church for years. The choir and the ministers and the acolytes would mill around in the cloakroom at 9:59 and Boomer'd say, "Okay, let's get the show on the road, folks," and get 'em lined up. And there were a few substitute pastors who'd feel Boomer's hand on their shoulder and hear him say, "C'mon, get your butt in line." Boomer hated the processional, fought against it. Hated having the entrance clogged with people in white dresses. Saw no reason why they had to parade up the aisle with candles. Boomer had a fire extinguisher in back, and he was ready to use it if a candle got dropped. He also hated the Exchange of Peace after the Prayer of Forgiveness. People getting up out of their seats and roaming around and shaking hands. It seemed disorderly to him.

Boomer got so he would have a little talk with the pastor after the service. Tell him, "We were ten minutes long today. Had two people leave early." He always said "we"—to him, it was a partnership. Finally, Boomer had to go. He was wearing shoes with flashing lights in the soles—so people could follow him more easily, he said—so the church gave him a recognition banquet, at which Boomer seemed not to remember people's names—he was seventy-two—and two weeks later, he and Sandy sold their house and left town and went to St. Cloud and, so we hear, became Methodists.

But he was the founder of the Herdsmen, and they still work from that 4-3-2 formation, even as other ushers have gone to a zone, and their secret still is quickness and anticipation. You can't push when you usher—that's called interference—and you can't close your hand over someone's arm—that's called holding—but those guys could move people. The National Church Acolytes & Assistants Association, the NC-Triple A, sponsored the National Ushers Competition, which was held at the Grand Opera House, which is a tough room to work—big balcony, three aisles, boxes, but that's where the Herdsmen went for the competition.

They raised money for the trip with a series of fish fries, and when you put on fish fries, you're going to gain weight, so they had to have their pants let out. They wear blue polyester suits with an *H* and a sheep embroidered on the pocket. They sat in nine adjoining seats in rows twenty-five, twenty-six, and twenty-seven, wedged in like marshmallows, and it was a turbulent flight down to Houston, especially on the descent; the plane was shaking hard, and steam or something was coming out of the vents, the wings were flapping, and they could hear the flight attendants in back singing "I Walk in the Garden Alone," which was not reassuring. But they landed in Houston, and then they got on a little bus, one of those buses that is a box set on a truck chassis, so the ride is much the same as what animals get en route to the stockyards, and the bus driver rode around lost, and when the Herdsmen arrived they were nauseated and dizzy. It was 1:30 and they were up to compete at two o'clock, so they barely had time to throw on their clothes, and it was a motley crowd. A thousand people and there were a lot of Episcopalians in there, and they always take more time, and a group of blind nuns, the Sisters of Helen Keller, and that slowed things up—old ladies waving white canes and whacking people with them, and some guide dogs growling and barking—and there were 140 members of Lutheran Weightwatchers, and the kids from St. Vitus's School for children with ADD, kids who come with a fast-forward button—it was like herding fruit bats and water buffalo. And there were only twenty stalls at the Communion rail and six servers, two of them elderly, but the Herdsmen got the job done by dividing people up and putting the elderly into another line, the sippers (who insist on drinking from the cup) in one line, and then three express lines for dippers—and they set a new national record, one thousand people taking Communion in fifteen minutes, about 1.1 second per communicant. They might've won first place, but two judges marked them low on style, which may have been due to indigestion from that bus ride. Both Elmer and Danny cut some cheese during the competition, loud ones, and the smell hung around, and you lose points for that.

Came home Friday, couldn't wait to tell people, and the nine of them marched into the Chatterbox Café for lunch and sat at the corner booth, all smiling and proud, and there was Dorothy, all steamed up over something, her hairnet loose. "Look at this," Dorothy said. She was reading the paper. A woman in Little Falls, fifty-two, followed her fifty-eight-year-old husband to the apartment of a woman, twenty-two, whom he had been seeing and who police said was pregnant by him. The wife burst in with a shotgun and fired both barrels at her husband as he tried to climb out the window. He was taken to the hospital with buckshot wounds in his ankle.

"Ankle! How can you fire both barrels at a man from fifteen feet away and just hit him in the ankle?" Dorothy looked around at the Herdsmen drinking their coffee. "How could you fire at a man with a shotgun and not kill him? I don't get it. How big a bedroom could it be? You got a naked guy climbing out a window fifteen feet away and you can't blow his head off? What's wrong with women nowadays?"

Mr. Berge smiled at her. "Maybe she loved him, despite everything. Maybe it was a warning shot."

Dorothy hooted. "A warning shot! The man was past warning! He was in the henhouse eating the chickens! She must've been using an old rusty gun. Men lock up the good ones, so the one she found was probably some old peashooter. No, she wanted to kill him—of course she did. I know I would." She looked down the row of Herdsmen. "If my husband had left me and had a baby with some tootsie, you bet I'd blow his head off. And no jury would convict me, either."

"We just got back from Houston," Elmer said. "We won first runner-up in the national contest." He set the trophy down on the counter.

"What's that, a bowling trophy?" she said.

"We were first runner-up in the National Ushers Competition at the Houston Grand Opera House on Thursday night."

"Well, aren't you special. What you going to have?"

"The usual for me," Elmer says.

And she reaches down and pinches the fat of his upper arm and waggles it and says, "I think maybe we've been having the usual too long, honey."

That's the recognition you get.

The argument about the wife who shot the husband in the ankle petered out, and Elmer strolled over with a picture of the National Ushers Hall of Fame that is going to be built in Houston. An architect's drawing, people strolling on a promenade, a garden of memories, and a Wall of Heroes where Boomer's picture would be. One of the greatest ushers who ever walked an aisle.

Dorothy looked at it for two seconds. "What's the big deal about that?"

Boomer's going to be in here. Hall of Fame in Houston. And the Herdsmen. A thousand people through Communion in fifteen minutes. A national record.

She looked at him as if he had a geranium growing out of his forehead. "What's the point of that?" she said.

Elmer sat down and had more coffee with the others. He thought maybe he'd give up ushering in church. Let somebody else have the grief. His wife died a year ago. Ovarian cancer. So he eats out. A lot. He misses her a lot and especially at night, just after he climbs into bed. There's no one there to tell about the ushering competition in Houston and how well they did, a thousand people in fifteen minutes, if only he hadn't cut one. Elmer thinks he'll quit the Herdsmen right after Easter. Of course, the time he was laid up with a bad knee and had to sit through the service and listen to the sermon, he sort of got discouraged about church. Hadn't heard a sermon for twenty years. The ushers always took that time to go over any last-minute changes in formation. Listening to the sermon made him feel he was in the wrong place. But he'll just have to get used to it.

*We're not called on to be attractive. Jesus didn't say,*
*"Blessed are the handsome and the witty and the well-informed."*
*Jesus said, "Blessed are they who mourn, for they shall be comforted."*

# 16

# Church Directory

I t has been a quiet week in Lake Wobegon. It's been warm, in the fifties, and got up to seventy on Thursday, and people have been raking their yards and digging in the flower beds, unwrapping their rosebushes. Of course, next week we could get eighteen inches of snow and be on the national news—"Midwest Lashed by April Blizzard"—that's the beauty of living in Minnesota, the constant sense of possibility. That's what makes a warm sunny day at the end of March so amazing. People stood in their shirtsleeves holding the end of a rake and looked over the fence at each other and grinned. Quite a day.

Pastor Ingqvist was not out raking. He and his wife, Judy, were having an argument in the kitchen. His sermon last Sunday was a real stink bomb. It was entitled "God, I'm Hungry," and he wrote it Saturday morning in a white heat of inspiration, and when he read it from the pulpit Sunday morning, he wanted to weep for how dumb it was, how pretentious, and he left out a lot of it, and afterward, about six people came up and said it was the best sermon they'd ever heard.

He said to her, "How could you let me give a sermon as lousy as that? 'God, I'm Hungry.' You typed it for me. Didn't you read it?"

"Yes, I did. I thought it was a little dumb, but—"

"Why did you let me go ahead and do it?"

"You're not an easy person to offer criticism to."

"Me? You're saying I can't take criticism? I can't believe you'd say that. Of course I can take criticism."

Members of the Luther League went door to door Thursday selling copies of the latest church directory, raising money to help send
the club to Bible camp in July. It costs $10 and includes the names
and birth dates of all the members of Lake Wobegon Lutheran and
pictures of all the families who attended church during Advent and
posed for their picture, including Pastor Ingqvist and his wife, Judy,
and daughter, Kate, and his boys, James and Andrew. Pastor Ingqvist
was just about to sneeze as the picture was taken, and his face is sort of
in transition, his mouth is making a little O, his eyes are half shut. He
looks snooty. He looked at his picture and his face burned. How could
they print such a thing?

It's a hard sell in a town where everybody pretty much knows everybody else already to the extent that they'd want to, and when the
Leaguers went around and made their pitch, quite a few people said,
"Well, let me think about that, and if I decide to get one, I'll give you
a call," which in Lake Wobegon means "No."

And some of the pictures . . . Lutherans generally avoid personal
vanity—they're like elm trees in that regard. But some of the pictures
were so unflattering, you couldn't help but notice. Daryl and Marilyn
Tollerud had their faces screwed up as if someone had sprayed them
with pepper. Virginia and Hjalmar Ingqvist looked as if they had just
spent thirty-six hours in an airport terminal. Mrs. Hoglund the organist looked as if she had been in a hostage situation, held prisoner in the
hold of a fishing boat, sleeping on piles of halibut. There were very few
faces that showed any joy at all, and what might have been joy, or felt
like joy to the person behind the face, appeared in the photographs to
be a kind of imbecility. Mr. and Mrs. Berge looked as if they should be
institutionalized right away and not allowed to operate motor vehicles. The Rasmussens appeared to be under heavy medication. Mr. and
Mrs. Wold had strange smiles on their faces that suggested they were
about to get on a plane for Argentina with every penny from the building fund. And most people in the book looked as if they should go on a
water and celery diet and do low-impact aerobics for six months.

Pastor Ingqvist bought a copy from his son Andrew, who is twelve,
and looked at the pictures and thought they looked pretty tacky, and
then he looked at his and he looked so hideous, he thought, *Is this meant*

*as satire? Are the kids putting us on here?* His daughter, Kate, worked on the directory. Kate is seventeen, the oldest child, sweet Kate—she used to get straight A's in school, and then last spring she got some new friends, and her average dropped a little bit, and she started to ask if she could bleach her hair. And then in November, she came home from an overnight, and she was a blonde. David and Judy didn't say a thing about it. A week went by, and no comment. They smiled at her and said, "Good morning, dear. Did you sleep well?" And one morning Kate said, "I'm getting my ears pierced." And Judy burst into tears and ran upstairs.

Was the directory a form of revenge? The Luther League getting back at their parents for all the times they'd been kept home on a Saturday night?

"Interesting pictures," Pastor Ingqvist said to Kate one morning.

"Oh?" she said. "What do you mean?"

She was wearing a blue angora sweater and a beige skirt, and her bleached hair was cut short. She used to look like Katharine Hepburn and now she looks like Madonna in her bimbo phase.

"How did you select the pictures?"

"I didn't."

"Who did?"

"Why? Is something wrong?"

"No, no. Just curious."

"By the way," she said, "when you flush the toilet upstairs, water comes out of the showerhead."

"I'll take a look at it," he said.

Pastor Ingqvist looked at the picture again. Kate looked okay, a little edgy the way teenagers do when they are caught in the company of their family, and Judy looked fairly pleasant. James had his eyes closed. And Andrew was looking straight into the camera and smiling. Amazing. It was so seldom this kid ever made eye contact.

Andrew is a big reader and the family doesn't have a lot of information on him yet. He's a mysterious child. He comes down in the morning with a book in hand, and it's hard to get much out of him. His mother puts breakfast in front of him and he eats it, in a detached way, like a robot, while reading, and his mother says, "Andrew, Daddy and I have decided to send you to military school in Germany. We think it'd be good for you. Daddy and I are moving to Nepal and switching to Buddhism. We've felt something missing in our lives, and we read a little bit about Buddhism and it seems like the thing for us, so Daddy is changing his name to 'Joyful Anticipation' and I'm going to become 'Serene Wisdom,' but you can just call me 'Whiz.' Okay, pal?" And the boy says, "Okay," and his eyes do not leave the page. If they want to communicate with him, they'll have to write a book, evidently.

Pastor Ingqvist went to his office Friday morning and asked Mrs. Lindorff if she knew about the pictures in the directory. Mrs. Lindorff is the volunteer secretary. They used to have a part-time paid secretary, but she left for a better job and Mrs. Lindorff came in as a full-time volunteer, and how do you say no to free help?

Mrs. Lindorff is in her mid-sixties, a big woman with helmet hair, and she looks very imposing in the directory, like Margaret Thatcher. Mrs. Lindorff said, "Well, you remember, Mr. Agar took them. Why? Is something wrong with them? I liked the one of you."

He poured himself a cup of her terrible coffee and went into his office and sat down. The paneling on the wall is coming loose in a couple of places. Most of the furniture in the room was donated, and one look at it tells you why they wanted to get rid of it. He pulled out a legal pad to start writing his sermon, and he drew some boxes at the top and drew lines connecting them. He thought he should say something about Lent, seeing as how it's coming to an end.

He looked at the directory again. His picture. That goofball face. What if somebody wanted to talk to him about a spiritual problem and they went to the directory to look up his number and thought, *Do I want to talk about my soul to a dumbo like that?*

That look on his face—he remembered where he'd seen that before—it was a Sunday morning and Val Tollefson had fallen asleep and everyone could hear him breathing out his mouth and the ushers came around with the offering plate and he woke up and there was a man with a tray and he said, "Another screwdriver." Everyone heard him and there were titters and Val got that goofy look on his face that Pastor Ingqvist had in the directory.

Well, we're not called on to be attractive. Jesus didn't say, "Blessed are the handsome and the witty and the well-informed."

Jesus said, "Blessed are they who mourn, for they shall be comforted."

He thought of calling up Mr. Agar and asking about the pictures.

Mr. Agar moved to town last summer. He's a teacher in the grade school. A nice man. Presbyterian, but here he is in a Lutheran town, so he changed to the cheaper brand. Mr. Agar has come in several times to discuss his spiritual life with Pastor Ingqvist, or rather his lack of one, which evidently is something that Presbyterians do, go talk to their ministers. Lutherans would rather walk naked through the streets than go see a minister about a thing like that, but Mr. Agar comes in and slumps down and says, "I don't know what's wrong with me, but I feel so listless, so empty—I read my Bible and I don't feel anything. I see the words and it doesn't seem to go in. Sometimes I wonder if I have any faith at all. I'm running on empty. What can you suggest for me?"

And Pastor Ingqvist says all the things a pastor should say—it's common to feel empty; God has promised to fill us with good things, but we have to wait on him, and meanwhile we simply stay busy and pray and look out for others and keep a cheerful heart—and what he wants to say is, "Hey, that's life. Get a grip."

He looked up Mr. Agar's picture in the directory. Mr. Agar has deep-set eyes, and he looks straight into the camera, he and his wife, both of them very thin people, and they both look as if they want to be your best friend.

And then he looked up and Mr. Agar was there. Mr. Agar was in distress. He closed the door behind him. Mr. Agar said, "I just looked at the directory. I feel sick. It's the wrong pictures. It's a digital camera. I guess I downloaded them wrong. I can't believe I could have goofed up like that. Those weren't the pictures I chose at all. What can I do to make it up to people?"

Pastor Ingqvist smiled at him. "What's the problem?" he said. "I thought the pictures were fine."

Mr. Agar said, "You didn't think yours was a little off-kilter?" He opened the directory to the Ingqvist family picture and squinted at it.

"I mean, that isn't the one I meant to use of you. I mean, you look— I don't know—like you weren't quite ready."

"That's how I look," said Pastor Ingqvist. "That's just me. You did the best you could and you captured me. Nothing wrong with that."

*The pastor read the story of Jesus and the woman who was being stoned, and he talked about forgiveness and said that the refusal to forgive freezes us in the ice of the past and we become fossils of our own pride.*

# 17

# Lorraine Turnblad's Tombstone

It has been a quiet week in Lake Wobegon, my hometown. This was the week we got our annual late March heartbreaker blizzard. Just when you're starting to imagine spring and crocuses and tulips, fourteen inches of snow fall and the temperature drops to ten below—it's a personally enriching experience you could do without; it's the equivalent of heading into the last mile of the marathon and tripping on your shoelace, falling, and breaking your leg.

School was not canceled. Everyone tuned in to *The Top of the Morning Show with Toivo and Ole* and they told a lot of jokes and then said, "Schools will be open today, but no bus service." Thus throwing the problem into the laps of parents. If you look out and think you can make it, then you drive them to school, and we are a people who are bred and raised to believe, *Yes, we can make it*, so except for a few pupils with sensible parents, everyone came to school. It was full of moody students and owly teachers.

Bud Mueller got out the plow and made a pass at clearing the streets. Most people didn't bother to shovel their walks. Pastor Ingqvist shoveled the walk in front of Lake Wobegon Lutheran—Mr. Hackl, the custodian, has been taking some sick days since the church board voted against his pay raise. He's pretty bitter. When you're unappreciated in your present job and you're unqualified for anything better, it does make a man resentful.

It was a slow day at church, and Pastor sat and studied the note that someone had put in the collection basket. In a sealed envelope, a card with hand-painted flowers said, "More and more, I look forward to Sunday morning when my being communes with your being, and my wholeness finds completeness in your wholeness, and I simply want you to know that you are loved and cherished by a stranger, more than you ever know."

It gave him the creeps to read it. Was it from the woman who is having the affair with the man in Duluth? Or Mrs. Tollefson, who used to drop by every week and want to talk about her empty marriage? Or the social studies teacher who stopped in one morning and said she could tell from looking at him in the pulpit that his body polarity was skewed and he really needed body work and could she show him what a simple neck and foot massage could do?

He was horrified at the thought. Lutheran pastors don't accept neck and foot massages from the flock. Lutherans are not a touching, stroking, feeling type of people; a handshake goes a long way with a Lutheran. Once we get to know you in thirty years or so, we might hug occasionally, but only sideways. Full frontal hugging is not natural to us, just as we don't spontaneously burst out into Puccini arias.

The teacher came around the desk in the pastor's study. "Just take off your shoes," she said. He stood up. He went around the other side of the desk. He said, "Do you smell smoke? I think I smell smoke. Excuse me." And then he went out the door and down the stairs and into the furnace room where Mr. Hackl likes to sit and read salacious literature. Mr. Hackl looked up. He was holding a copy of *Life* magazine with a picture on the cover of the Milky Way taken by the Hubble telescope, but inside it he had another magazine. Pastor Ingqvist pulled up a chair. He said, "I thought it was time we went over our plan for re-seeding the lawn this year."

Two robins arrived on Tuesday; they landed in Arlene Bunsen's backyard and they seemed to be not getting along. They were pecking at each other and screeching, and he would try to land on a branch by her and she'd attack him and he'd fly away, though eventually they settled down. I suppose you've had trips like that yourselves. To leave the

South and come all this way to Minnesota, because it is a better place to raise children—that's why all the birds come—and to arrive and find a foot of snow and bitter winds and cold—it's enough to make a bird question its own instincts and to ask, *How can we robins bring children into a world so cruel as this?*

But spring is coming. The Sons of Knute is holding its annual Ice Melt Contest and the old '49 jalopy is parked on the ice by the skating rink, a chain around its rear axle, and for $1 you can guess the day and the hour it will finally fall through. Mid to late April is a good guess, though it has gone earlier, and a few years ago it was still there in the middle of May. Some joker had put air bags in it. They suspected Denny Pfleiderscheidt because he's pulled some fast ones in the past and he had guessed May 15, so this seemed to have Pfleiderscheidt written all over it.

"How would I have gone out there while the ice was soft and stuck air bags in there?" he said.

They said, "We were hoping you'd tell us."

He said, "I don't know a thing about it."

They said, "Well, you put May 15 down on this slip of paper."

"Oh," he said, "well, maybe I meant March."

The prize was $225, but they wouldn't give him the money. They said, "The contest was to guess when the car goes through the ice, not how long it can float on water." So all the money went into the Sons of Knute Shining Star Scholarship Fund that sends bright but well-behaved young people away to college, none of whom ever seem to come back here to live, and that's why there are proportionally so many Denny Pfleiderscheidts in Lake Wobegon. Sending bright people away to college doesn't seem to be in our best interests somehow—giving young people opportunities for further education tends to make them less useful to us—but education is one of our ideals, and I'm afraid we're stuck with it.

There was a little procession up in the cemetery on Wednesday, through the snow. Bud plowed the road into the cemetery so cars could park there, and Pastor Ingqvist led the procession—there were eight people, six from town and an old man and an old woman who'd come up from Chicago—and they trudged out into the snow up to a spot where it had been shoveled away from a grave where a stone lay that said, "Lorraine Turnblad, 1897–1918." It was a new stone. The old woman was Lorraine Turnblad's niece, and she wanted the stone blessed, which Pastor Ingqvist agreed to do out of compassion, though Lutherans don't bless headstones—they're not inclined to view places or objects as sacred. A few years ago, the snowmobile club wanted him to take part in the Blessing of the Snowmobiles, which is a tradition at Our Lady of Perpetual Responsibility. Every year, with the first good snowfall, a hundred of them come roaring up to Our Lady Church and Father Wilmer comes out and blesses them and prays, "O thou who didst teach us that here on Earth we are but pilgrims, bless these thy servants on the snow that these machines may be used safely and for thy glory," and then they roar off to the Moonlite Bay Resort and drink boilermakers. Well, Pastor Ingqvist refused to take part, said he couldn't see snowmobiles as sacred, which caused some hard feelings, but he agreed to do this headstone, and then he asked his wife, Judy, "What am I going to do?"

She said, "These people are Episcopalians, so maybe they'd like some water sprinkled," and she got a tall saltshaker with a silver cap and put water in it and they brought that.

Lorraine Turnblad was a beautiful Lake Wobegon girl who in 1917, at the age of twenty, suddenly married a young soldier who was about to leave for France. She was very pregnant at the time, and it was such a disgrace to the family that her father would not attend the wedding or let anyone else in the family go to it, and that day passed and they sat down to supper with tears in their eyes, and he looked around the table with tears in his and he said, "I will never hear her name spoken in this house again. Take it as a lesson that God is not mocked and some things you shall not do."

The young soldier took her to Minneapolis where she lived with his aunt, and she was struck down in the great influenza epidemic of 1918 and died alone, her unborn child dying with her, and her body was sent home and was buried by the county under a con-crete marker with only a number on it. The young soldier didn't come back from the war. Nobody knew what happened to him. The father never visited Lorraine's grave. He said, "Let her lie there. She made her choice, and let her have it," and when he died, he was buried at the other end of the cemetery. And now, all these years later, here was Lorraine's niece from Chicago, Lois, trying to make things right.

She had called the courthouse, and they looked around in the records and said Lorraine's grave was number 77. And she called the Made Rite Monument Company in St. Cloud and told them what inscription she wanted, and they brought the stone to the cemetery and set the stone down where there was a metal marker, 77, in the ground under a spreading oak tree. Lois thought that by the end of March it'd be green up there, but it snowed instead, so there they were, up to their knees in snow, Pastor Ingqvist trying to invent a ritual over a granite headstone with "Lorraine Turnblad, 1897–1918" on it, and the message "Let Him Who Is without Sin Cast the First Stone"—which the man at the monument factory heard on the phone as "Let Him Who Is with Oxen Cast the First Stone," which might make sense to people who've had oxen but didn't to him, so he called the church and got it straightened out.

They didn't tell Lois about that, and they didn't tell her what the county clerk, Viola Tors, told Pastor Ingqvist. She said, "I didn't know what to say to that woman. Those records disappeared years ago. I had no idea where her aunt was, but I thought, heck, one unmarked grave is pretty much like another, and I remembered that 77 was sort of in a pretty place, and why not." So it became the Tomb of the Unknown Sinner. The pastor read the story of Jesus and the woman who was being stoned, and he talked about forgiveness and said that the refusal to forgive freezes us in the ice of the past and we become fossils of our own pride. That was when Lois's husband brought out a boom box from under his coat and held it up high in the air and played a tape of the Mormon Tabernacle Choir singing "Abide with Me," and Judy Ingqvist looked up and saw Mr. Halvorson, her old enemy, the superintendent of schools, standing next to Lois, who is his aunt—he is a Turnblad on his mother's side—and she looked at him and tried to forgive him.

She's fought with him hard. Everything they do in schools nowadays is purely to save money. Everything. They stagger the start times so that one set of buses serves high school, middle school, and elementary, and high school kids are the first load. High school starts at 7:00 a.m. The kids come in like stunned cattle, and they get an education that the school has cut down to nothing. They cut Latin and German, cut trigonometry and plane geometry, hired a fool to teach physics who has no degree in it, cut art and music, and history is mostly taught by coaches who have their students spend the class period reading a chapter of the textbook and then taking an easy multiple choice test, while the coach sits and reads the sports page.

Judy looked at him, tears running down his cheeks, and she thought, *I can forgive a lot of things, but I still have a couple of stones I'd like to throw at this bozo.*

They stood in the cemetery, thinking of that lovely girl and how she probably met that soldier on a summer night, at a dance, and how handsome he looked in his uniform, his cap, his leggings, his shiny boots, and how she might have felt that her life had opened up and someone loved her, and she thought, *I can't say no to something I've waited so long for.* So she seized love and she was destroyed.

And the hymn ended, and he pressed the stop button on the boom box, and Judy handed David the saltshaker and he flung the water down on the grave that might have held Lorraine or might have held someone else, some pauper, some bum who fell off a train, some infant found in a garbage can who never had a name, somebody else the county buried—he flung the water down and gave the saltshaker to the niece, and she flung some, and her husband did, and they all took a turn, throwing salty drops like tears onto the stone, where they froze.

Pastor Ingqvist went back to his office, feeling depressed, and found his office was fifty-two degrees, and got Mr. Hackl up from the furnace room where he was studying young women in bathing suits. He looked at the thermostat and said, "Not much I can do. Whole system needs to be replaced if you ask me. But hey, what do I know? Not much, according to some people," and then he hit the wall under the thermostat with his fist, hard, and they could hear the furnace start up down below and feel the hot air come out the vent.

*You can never break your connection to people you love.*
*You may think you do, and years may pass, and you never think of them,*
*but they always return to you.*

# 18

# The Pastor's Résumé

It has been a quiet week in Lake Wobegon. Holy Week. Pastor Ingqvist worked on his sermon. He saw a line in *Sanctity Fair*, the pastoral magazine, that said, "A sermon should have a good beginning and a good end, and they should be as close together as possible." In his sermon, he says, "Some people will never understand right or wrong because they're so powerful that they think they get to decide. But God has another view of the matter, and that is what Passover and Easter make clear. God is God, and what God says goes. The Pharaoh lives in his vast palaces with their sumptuous gardens and immense monuments and statuary, and he is deluded by his own grandeur and believes that when he says no to Moses, that is the last word, and it isn't. God has not spoken. God will speak."

It was cold and cloudy and dark and depressing most of this week. People sat in the Chatterbox and read gloomy tales in the newspaper, read them out loud—"Look at this. A man went berserk on a golf course in Hawaii and clubbed his foursome to death with a No. 3 iron." And there were long boring conversations about the comparative prices of building materials—"Yeah, they got the three-quarter-inch Sheetrock down at Menard's about four cents cheaper, I hear. I might have to drive over and look at that." And the trees are bare and the grass is brown and the people are owly. You drive north up around Millet, you see a slew of No Trespassing signs—and not the printed ones, but ones with steel letters individually nailed into a piece of plywood, and you can see that the guy who pounded in the letters hit them hard enough to splinter the plywood—a driveway you would never drive up looking for directions. All of us are owly. Dorothy has a sign up over the cash register saying, "This Is Not a Real Job. This Is Only a Test. Had This Been a Real Job, You Would Have Received a Raise, a Promotion, and Other Signs of Appreciation."

But by April, we're used to cold weather and we've learned to look on the bright side. I met a distinguished man in Los Angeles once who told me that the climate of the Midwest is not conducive to a modern lifestyle, and that's why the Midwest has declined economically past the point of return and is now effectively a colony. He said, "You've lost your population base, and with that comes an inevitable loss of economic vitality. And that is why Midwestern culture is dying, because it takes an expanding economy to support a culture." He said, "Look at Renaissance Florence. Look at London, Paris, New York. Business is what creates art." What made this interesting to me was the fact that his pants were unzipped. I don't think he knew that, or if he did, he didn't refer to it. And one advantage of the Minnesota climate is that you always know if your fly is unzipped. That may not seem enough justification for cold weather, but I would rather know than not know.

There was a going-away lunch at the Chatterbox for Clint Bunsen's son, Lawrence, who is twenty-two and moving to California. It's too cold for him here, he says, and he wants to move before he gets too settled. He's worked at Bunsen Motors for two years, and they're not so sad to see him go. Lawrence is enormously strong but not mechanically gifted, which is a bad combination. He's taken the lug nuts off a tire so hard the car came crashing down off the jack. He'd check your oil and ram the stick right out the bottom of the oil pan and close the hood so hard he'd be holding the hood ornament in his hand. Once, Clint had him drive a car onto the grease rack, and he got it on the rack but then stomped on the brake and missed and hit the accelerator, and the car shot ahead into the tool chests, and there was oil and antifreeze everywhere, and the car with its back end up on the rack, the grille smashed in. Shelves bent. Being a child of one of the owners, he had job security, but for two years they've had to keep an eye on him and to anticipate disaster and to practice preventive management.

They sent him off with a glowing recommendation. Our revenge on the West Coast.

That was on Wednesday he left. And then on Thursday the sun came out and it was warm and bright, and on Thursday night there was a full moon so bright you could see your shadow, and on Friday the sun came out again.

There was a big Good Friday service at Our Lady of Perpetual Responsibility yesterday, and Father Wilmer gave a good homily on the value of suffering as a bringer of truth. Afterward, Myrtle Krebsbach stood outside the door and hugged her friends as she saw them come out—Myrtle has suddenly been exhibiting hugging tendencies, and it's made people nervous because many of them are still mad at her from her pre-hugging days when she used to be so mean. Myrtle is in her seventies, and she goes around in a purple pantsuit and a jet-black wig, leaving a smoke trail of profanity behind her, which used to embarrass her grandchildren to tears—to hear their grandma swear like a sailor. This is not a sailing town. She insulted a lot of people, told them off to their faces, walked up and berated people on the street. And then she turned into a hugger.

Mrs. Magendanz came out the door and Myrtle sprang toward her, arms outstretched: "Oh, Sylvia, isn't it wonderful? Wasn't it good? The peace of Christ, Sylvia. God bless you."

And to Myrtle's daughter Eloise, the mayor of Lake Wobegon: "Oh, honey, I look at you and I just thank God, I'm so lucky. The peace of Christ. God bless you."

Eloise was stunned. Her mother had never said that before. Her mother used to say, "If you get any bigger . . ."

Myrtle didn't put her arms around Florian, her husband. She drew the line there. She didn't want him to get ideas. But she hugged Father Wilmer: "Oh, Father, let me give you a hug." And he did. Though he didn't give her much of a squeeze.

Myrtle got a letter last week from a boy she used to be in love with. The first boy she ever loved. She showed it to her granddaughter, Sue Ann, Carl's girl. Myrtle was weeping. "He was the sweetest boy. He was the only one who liked to dance, and he liked to sing. He and I would sit on the porch and sing all the songs we knew. He was in love with me, and my brothers thought he was too strange, and they ran him off. And I didn't stand up for him like I should've. It's a terrible thing to let people be mean to someone you love. It cheapens you. He came to the house late one night and threw gravel at my window, and I snuck down to talk to him. We stood in the yard and I could tell he'd been hurt. They'd hit him. He put his arms around me and he said, 'I love you so much. I don't know what'll happen to me without you.' I didn't say anything. We kissed, and he went away and I never saw him again. And now he's sick and dying and I can't go see him." And she cried. Sue Ann looked at the letter and realized that this boy is now seventy-eight. And to Myrtle it was like yesterday.

The Lutheran women's softball team was out at the ballpark, shagging flies and scooping up grounders, and when you looked at the coach in his old letter jacket hitting those fungos, you were surprised to see Pastor Ingqvist. He never used to coach, and as you watch him you can see why he didn't. He got that letter for pole-vaulting, not softball. But he's making an effort. He got a little mad at the congregation in January after he and Judy got schnookered out of their trip to Orlando to the ministerial retreat. The money was in the budget, $1,800, but Val Tollefson stood up at a board meeting and said he felt they ought to be doing more for Rwanda, and he passed around pictures of horror and suffering, and what could a minister say? Hard to defend spending that money on a week by a pool under the palms surrounded by tight, tanned bodies when there is such need in the world. So the $1,800 went to relief, and the pastor sulked and studied the Pastors Wanted column in *Sanctity Fair* magazine, and in February he sent off his résumé to Texas.

It was hard to come up with a résumé after twenty years in the same job—"1975 to present: Senior Pastor, Lake Wobegon Lutheran Church. Responsibilities include: weekly sermon (samples enclosed), counseling, comforting, special events including baptisms, weddings, and funerals, plus daily prayer and meditation." He sent the résumé to the Dallas/Fort Worth Airport, which had advertised for a chaplain. A vice president of the airport management company, a guy named Don, called him back on the phone and said they were tripling their chapel capacity at DFW because, he said, "We're trying to promote a concept of community here. We want people to see DFW as a destination in itself." He said, "A lot of people move around so much they never establish a church home, and because you've got to stay over Saturday to get the cheaper rates, lots of folks don't get home Sunday morning. We think the chapel at DFW can serve those people. Pastor Ingqvist, from what I can see, you fit the bill perfectly. You're just the man we're looking for." It paid $85,000 a year plus some kind of profit-sharing, which clergy so seldom get.

They flew him down there for an interview. He sat next to a beautiful woman who fell asleep, and her head came to rest on his shoulder, and her long black hair flowed across his face—it smelled so good. He did not attempt to wake her up. And as the plane made its descent, he could see dark clouds just below them, and then they were in the clouds, and the plane bucked and rolled, and it shook, and people behind him were sobbing, calling out the names of loved ones. A man across the aisle was writing as fast as he could on a legal pad. A woman was weeping, and a flight attendant said, "Can I bring you a glass of water?" and the woman said, "Yes, and a cyanide capsule, please." The beautiful woman on his shoulder slept away. Pastor Ingqvist realized that he was the Jonah on this ship. In the Bible, Jonah tries to escape God's will by sailing away on a ship, and God sends a terrible storm as a reminder. Pastor Ingqvist said a prayer. He said, "Please let us land safely. I get the message. I will stay there, even if they are a bunch of flatheads." And then the plane was hit from below, and hit so hard that the oxygen masks tumbled down into their laps. He grabbed his and put it on the sleeping woman's face, and just as she woke up, he felt the wheels rolling along beneath. They'd touched down and bounced. She smiled at him sleepily. She said, "Are we there?"

A young woman from the airport management company met him and gave him a two-hour tour of the Dallas/Fort Worth Airport. She was tremendously proud of the place, though she'd been there only three months—her young life had somehow found fulfillment there at the airport. He was taken to the chapel to wait for the vice president. There were soft pews and an altar in front, and above it hung a large Lucite ball, backlit, and two candles, and a book that lay open. He looked around for a cross but there was none, just the ball.

Interdenominational, evidently. He stepped up front and looked at the book, expecting it to be a Bible, but it wasn't: it was called *The Book of Wisdom*, and it was sort of a spiritual Yellow Pages, alphabetical by problem: words of wisdom when troubled by Adultery; Anger; Betrayal, Feelings of; Business Failure; Covetousness; Criminal Indictments; Doubt—with a whole page of meaningless platitudes for each one.

He waited in the chapel for an hour, and he counted sixteen people who came in, people who sat in prayer, or knelt, their hands clutching the pew in front of them, tears running down their faces. A man saw him and asked, "Are you a minister?"

Pastor Ingqvist said, "Yes."

The man said, "I did a terrible thing. I left my family. I lied. I cheated. I'm so ashamed. I called my wife and we talked for six hours on the phone. She said she forgives me. I'm going back there in half an hour. God wouldn't kill me now, would he? God wouldn't do that?"

Pastor Ingqvist looked at him. He said, "God is all loving, and God is all wise."

The man seemed disappointed by this answer. He said, "Listen. I wrote a letter to my wife. Would you take it and mail it to her if the plane crashes?"

Pastor Ingqvist said, "There's a mailbox upstairs. Why not just mail it to her?"

The man said, "Because if I don't crash, I'm not sure I'd say it in just this way."

Pastor Ingqvist never got to meet the vice president. The young woman came and apologized, "He's been called off to a meeting, he is terribly sorry, we'll be in touch,"—and Pastor Ingqvist flew home. He was glad to get back. No matter the serious faults it has, and they are serious, home is a place where, when you get there, you know it. You can never separate yourself from the love of God; you can never separate yourself from home. You can never break your connection to people you love. You may think you do, and years may pass, and you never think of them, but they always return to you. Myrtle hadn't thought of that boy for years, and then this week she saw him clearly again: the boy her brothers had beaten up standing in the moonlight saying good-bye to her, and she didn't dare put her arms around him. Love can never be broken or discarded.

*If pride were kindling, our family could heat the church for twenty years.*

# 19

# The Yard of All Yards

Charlotte takes everything so personally. She's usually unhappy about something when she comes over. Somebody's done this, somebody's said that, they got no right to, and what makes them think they can get away with that? Once, Charlotte sat at the kitchen table and said, "I don't know what I'm going to do when you're gone," and cried, and Ella tried to comfort her. Strange. The dear departed comforting the survivor prior to departure.

Ella doesn't think about it herself. Not much. Not as much as she did thirty years ago.

She does think about visitors. She'd like some. Visitors Welcome. Free Coffee. Come In. No need to stay long. No need to tell the literal truth, either. She doesn't mind if you say you're doing fine when you're not. She just wants some company. Loneliness is so dramatic. It makes all your troubles seem big and tragic. Hers aren't. They're quite ordinary if she had some ordinary visitors. She's thinking of giving away free balloons, too. She'd like some business.

With a friend there, you could even talk about death and it would seem normal. Charlotte, she can't bear to hear about death without wanting to call an ambulance. But with a friend, you could say, simply, "I'm ready to die. I'm ready." And the friend would say, "That's good," and you'd look and see that the friend is death.

She told Pastor Ingqvist that on his regular Monday call. He said, "I'm glad to hear that." Then they went outside and raked the front. All the dead grass. And he summarized his sermon for her. It's warm now; she could go on Sunday and probably she will, but she likes home delivery, too. Then he had to go home and rake his own lawn.

Last Saturday, about lunchtime, the song of the rototiller was heard. Clarence Bunsen came out his front door, sandwich in hand, to see who it was—a number of people stuck their heads out. It was Lyle, plowing up his garden. Amazing. April 7. What was he doing that for? He can't plant anything for three weeks yet. Or can he? Has he discovered something we don't know?

Gardening is a competitive sport in Lake Wobegon. It's friendly, and people are generous with the produce—you want zucchini in August, you got it—but you sit around with people earlier in the summer, and you'll find out what a cutthroat business it is. You say, "Well, this is sure good tomato weather. Mine are starting to turn red already."

And they say, "Mmm-hmm. Well, let us give you some to take home. We got more than we can use right now."

And you say, "You have tomatoes? Already?"

And they say, "Oh sure. It's almost the end of June. We usually have tomatoes by Memorial Day."

You sit in silence. You'd like to say, "How do you do it?" But you're afraid they'll tell you. So instead you say, "Well, I never cared much for early tomatoes. They always taste mealy to me. Late tomatoes are juicier. I don't know." You do what you can to recover your pride, but it hurts when your garden gets beat out by theirs. It's as if you had said, "My kid won a driver training award from the Lions Club; he's going to Fargo next week to compete in a parallel-park-off," and they say, "Oh, that's nice. Todd and Jennifer just left for Vienna last week. They won a travel fellowship from Harvard to study international relations. They'll be there for a month and then go to Cairo, Bombay, Singapore, and Tokyo. It's an all-expense-paid fellowship. They give it to only four American high school students each year, and our kids just happened to win two of them." Then you are supposed to say, "That's great," but you don't because they know it's great—that's why they mentioned it. Somebody lays down four aces on your pair of threes, and you don't say, "Good hand"—they already know it. They're reaching for your money.

There are plenty of intensely competitive people in Lake Wobegon, and I don't mean the Whippets. Every spring when the Thanatopsis

Club puts on the annual lyceum and brings in a big out-of-town lecturer, the poor celebrity goes away with ugly red bruises on her, squeeze marks from all the Thanatopsians grabbing her and saying, "Come over here and sit down with us. Come here and meet my husband." Every spring there's a campaign at some homes to make the front yard truly outstanding, the yard of all yards. And then there's high school graduation. About six years ago, the school decided to cut out the speeches by the valedictorian, salutatorian, and class orator because they all sounded the same and because the school thought graduation should be fun and the student speakers usually were white around the gills and tended to sway at the podium. Well, that was the year Charlotte Holm made valedictorian and her cousin Helen was class orator, so the family thought this was an anti-Holm move. That was the year that the organic material hit the ventilating device. They wanted those children up in plain view with gold tassels and with words coming out of their mouths. And they got their way. Charlotte's speech was entitled "Service to Others," and it was based on Christ's words to the rich young man: "Give all that you have to the poor and follow me." It was good. The Holms thought it was the greatest speech ever given. Her dad didn't hear a word of it—he was all over the place taking 8mm movies. In color. Silent.

Well, you can forgive the Holms their pride, I guess, if you remember back to 1926. That was the year that Norwegian royalty visited Lake Wobegon, a major event, as you can imagine. Hjalmer Ingqvist's dad, Johnson Ingqvist, arranged this. He was a big contributor to the Republican party and knew the governor well enough that the governor had been to his home for coffee one afternoon. A hundred children stood out on the front lawn to watch him drink it, on a rainy day, and that lawn was never so outstanding after that; it had to be resodded. So when Mr. Ingqvist heard that King Haakon VII would be visiting Minnesota and taking a motor tour of Norwegian settlements, Mr. Ingqvist put in his bid with the governor and got the king for two hours, 2:30 to 3:45 (almost two hours), on May 14, 1926. The town learned about this in early April, and people just about killed themselves doing yard work. This was in the era of pretty casual lawns. Children played on them, and standards of turf maintenance were fairly low. Many lawns had a dirt pit in one corner where home plate was. Crabgrass was just another variety of grass. But when they imagined the king of Norway driving by, people got to work beautifying—even the German Catholics did.

The Germans pooh-poohed the whole thing at first. They pointed out that King Haakon VII wasn't even Norwegian; he was a Danish prince whom the Norwegian parliament had imported when Norway split off from Sweden in 1905, which technically was true. And this was America, where every person is as good as another, which technically is true, too. But when the good Norwegians of Lake Wobegon thought of the king coming to visit, they got so excited they had to sit down.

In Norway, their ancestors had been dirt poor and had never seen royalty, let alone hung around with them, so the king's visit was a sign that they had made good in America, accomplished things, could hold up their heads. At the same time, they had been so busy making good in America, they had started to forget old Norway, so the king's visit was like the past coming to greet them, as if your grandfather rose from the dead and came to shake your hand and say, "You done good. I'm proud."

They set to work making themselves worthy. They polished up their Norwegian. They bought new clothes. They painted. They fixed up. In 1926, most farmers came to town in wagons, so they cleaned up Main Street and said, "No more horses there until after the visit." They created a Lake Wobegon Norwegian children's choir where there had been none before, and drilled those forty children in six Norwegian songs. Those children now are almost seventy, and they still remember the words. And the Norwegians imagined how it would be. Each of them imagined the long black car pulling up in front of his house, and the tall man in the blue suit getting out and walking up to their door to visit, and the bows and the curtsies, and him sitting down at their table and having his krummkake and coffee and he says, "Smake saa god. Vaer saa god. Du er saa snille. Mange takk. Mange mange takk." "It tastes so good. Very good. You are so kind. Many thanks."

Then came the bad news. Mr. Ingqvist decided that since the visit would be so short and the king would be so busy on his trip and would be tired, the only sensible thing would be to give him a chance to lie down and rest. Why wear him out showing him things he'd seen and heard a thousand times before? A choir: How many children's choirs has he heard? How many times has he heard those same songs? No, the king deserved true hospitality. He'd come to town, sit a moment with the Ingqvists, and then go upstairs and have a nap. No choir, no band, no cheering crowds. Quiet. The king should have quiet.

To Mr. Ingqvist this was a simple, sensible, humane decision, and that was that. He'd invited the king, so there was no more to be said.

The bitterness, the hurt, the hard feelings that were created—you still find traces of them today, almost sixty years later. After Mr. Ingqvist made his decision, then Mrs. Ingqvist decided they would invite some of her family, the Tollefsons, to have a bite with the king before his nap, and then the Berges got in and the Olesons, and soon there were twelve people who would have coffee with the king and then sit very quietly downstairs while he rested, and there were several hundred who wouldn't, including many who felt they should, who had done well, who deserved this honor. The Ringnes family was devastated, Paul and Florence. They never forgave this insult. Paul never did business with Mr. Ingqvist again, which wasn't easy—Mr. Ingqvist owned the bank. Florence was so humiliated. She was Mrs. Ingqvist's cousin—they were best friends as girls—and those two didn't speak after that. It was soon after that Mrs. Ringnes began her career domineering the ladies' circle at church. She bossed every church supper and was so ferocious and sharp-tongued and terrifying that younger women literally could not butter bread or boil water in her presence. She was so superior, she made other people incompetent. It began with that insult, being left out of the king's visit.

And it didn't change matters much at all when, the day before the visit, the king got sick in Minneapolis and couldn't come. He'd been in America one week and had attended twelve lutefisk dinners and was resting in his suite at the Nicollet Hotel, attended by physicians from the Mayo Clinic. It was only three years since President Warren G. Harding had died from eating something on a tour, and the governor was horrified at the thought of the king expiring in Minnesota of an excess of hospitality, so he was put on toast and tea, and a Norwegian count named Count Carl was sent around in his place. Then Mr. Ingqvist changed his mind. Count Carl wouldn't be tired, so they could go ahead and have a big do, and they did, but that didn't change matters either. People were still mad.

Count Carl was a big bear of a man with heavy black eyebrows and a rumbling voice, and a good eater. They gave him a dinner at the Sons of Knute lodge, and he ate everything put before him. Then the children's choir sang their six songs, and with the first note of music, Count Carl's head fell to his chest and he slept the sleep of the innocent. He snored through the presentation and awoke with the applause and jumped up and took a bow. He spoke for five minutes in Norwegian, got in his car, and left. If he noticed how nice the yards looked, he didn't mention it to anybody.

This changed nothing. People were hurt, humiliated, by not being invited to meet the king. This hurt has diminished gradually as the people who weren't invited have died. Now almost all of them are dead.

Last week there was a little act of forgiveness that took place at Lake Wobegon Lutheran, in the basement, in the furnace room. Luther Ringnes, Florence's oldest son, came up from the Cities for the dedication of the new gas furnace that he donated to the church. It was installed last summer, but he only recently decided to name it for his parents, so he and Pastor David Ingqvist, who is the grandnephew of the Ingqvist who invited the king, held a small ceremony. They drilled four holes in the front above the little window that looks in at the pilot light and attached a simple brass plate: "The Paul and Florence Ringnes Memorial Furnace." Luther had a bottle of brandy. He poured a little into two Dixie cups and smashed the rest against the furnace. "Well," said Pastor Ingqvist, "I think you christened it. Tell me this," he said, "do you want an announcement in the church bulletin?"

"I don't know. What do you think? What do you think other people would think?"

"I suppose they would think it was funny. Naming a furnace after your parents. Not many people would do it, I suppose. Why did you do it, anyway?"

Luther thought. "My parents were the proudest people I've ever known. My mother wouldn't let even relatives in the house except on

Sunday when it was clean. My father drove forty miles to deposit his money because he didn't get invited to meet the king of Norway in 1926. If they could choose a memorial for themselves, I'm sure they'd prefer a bell, or a whole carillon, but I always thought if pride were kindling, our family could heat the church for twenty years. So . . ."

"Well," Pastor Ingqvist said, "if I dedicated the gas tank to the memory of my great-uncle, we'd have us a complete set. Here's to you, Luther. Good health." And they drank a toast and put the Dixie cups on the floor and smashed them underfoot and turned out the light and went to lunch, the brass plate to the memory of Paul and Florence above the window, and inside the furnace the little flame of the pilot light flickering. It was a good furnace all winter; they didn't have a single problem with it. It runs real quiet, and when you turn up the thermostat early Sunday morning, she goes from fifty to seventy in about an hour flat.

*"Be not conformed to this world: but be ye transformed."*

# 20

# Confirmation Sunday

Spring has come, grass is green, the trees are leafing out, birds are arriving every day by the busload, and now the Norwegian bachelor farmers are washing their sheets. In town the windows are open, so as you pause in your walk to admire Mrs. Hoglund's rock garden, you can smell her floor wax and hear the piano lesson she is giving, the tune that goes "da da Da da Da da da," and up by the school, you can smell the macaroni and cheese hotdish for lunch and hear from upstairs the voices of Miss Melrose's class reciting Chaucer.

> Whan that Aprill with his shoures soote
> The droghte of March hath perced to the roote,
> And bathed every veyne in swich licour
> Of which vertu engendred is the flour;
> Whan Zephirus eek with his sweete breeth
> Inspired hath in every holt and heeth
> The tendre croppes, and the yonge sonne
> Hath in the Ram his halve cours yronne,
> And smale foweles maken melodye
> That slepen al the nyght with open eye . . .

The words are six hundred years old and describe spring in this little town quite well; the sweet breath of the wind, the youth of the sun, the sweet rain, the tendre croppes, the smale fowles maken melodye: we have them all.

I made a pilgrimage up there last Sunday to visit my family, and my family wasn't there. I walked in, called; there was no answer.

I drove over to Aunt Flo's to look for them and got caught in Sunday morning rush hour. It was Confirmation Sunday at Lake Wobegon Lutheran Church. Thirteen young people had their faith confirmed and were admitted to the circle of believers, thirteen dressed-up boys and girls at the altar rail in front of a crowd of every available relative. Pastor Ingqvist asked them all the deepest questions about the faith (questions that have troubled theologians for years), which these young people answered readily from memory before partaking of their first Communion. Later they lounged around on the front steps and asked each other, "Were you scared?" and said, "No, I really wasn't, not as much as I thought I'd be," and went home to eat chuck roast, and some of them had their first real cup of coffee. They found it to be a bitter, oily drink that makes you dizzy and sick to your stomach, but they were Lutherans now and that's what Lutherans drink.

The Tolleruds, for example, drank gallons of coffee on Sunday. Church had been two hours long, the regular service plus confirmation, and Lutherans don't have the opportunity to stand up and kneel down and get exercise that you find elsewhere, so everyone was stiff and dopey, and the Tolleruds, when they sit around and visit, are all so quiet and agreeable they get drowsy, so they drink plenty of coffee. Years ago, when Uncle Gunnar was alive, they didn't need so much. He had wild white hair and eyebrows the size of mice, he spilled food on himself and didn't care, he had whiskey on his breath, and if anyone mentioned the Lutheran church, he said, "Haw!"

He was an old bachelor who got rich from founding a chain of private clubs in the Dakotas and Iowa called the Quality Prestige Clubs. They were only empty rooms over a drugstore with some old leather couches and a set of *Collier's Encyclopedia*, and he gave away memberships to men who'd never been invited to join a club before—tall, sad men with thin dry hair, of whom there are a lot—and made his money selling them lots of shirts and ties and cuff links with the QP insignia. Uncle Gunnar got rich and sold the clubs to an Iowa meatpacker and went to Australia to get into some line of work down there he didn't consider worth mentioning, and the last anyone saw him was in 1962. Presumably he died, unless perhaps he just got tired of us knowing him.

The Tolleruds gathered for pot roast because Daryl and Marilyn's daughter Lois was confirmed. She sat at the head of the table, next to her dad, promoted from the children's table out in the kitchen. She is a tall, lanky girl who has grown four inches this year, and it has tired her out. She is quieter than she used to be, a shy girl with long brown hair she has learned to tie in an elegant bun and creamy skin that she keeps beautiful by frequent blushing, which is good for the circulation and makes her lovelier whenever she is admired.

A boy who has sat silently across from her in geometry since September has written her a twenty-seven-page letter in small print telling her how he feels about her (since September he's looked as if he was just about to talk, and now it all comes out at once: he thinks God has written their names together in the Book of Love). But she wasn't thinking about him Sunday—she was blushing to see her confirmation cake with the Scripture verse inscribed in blue frosting: "Be not conformed to this world: but be ye transformed by the renewing of your mind, that ye may prove what is good, and acceptable, and perfect, that you may discern the will of God." It was a large cake, and Marilyn used the extra-fine nozzle on the frosting gun—there it sat, lit with birthday candles, and Lois didn't know how to tell them that she wasn't sure that she believed in God. She was pretty sure that she might've lost her faith.

She thought she might've lost it on Friday night or sometime Saturday morning; she wasn't sure. She didn't mention it at that time because she thought she might get it back.

On Friday night, less than forty-eight hours before confirmation, she was sitting on the couch watching television with Dave, the boy who wrote the letter, while her mom and dad were gone to have supper with her prayer parents. When you're confirmed, you're assigned prayer parents, a couple who promise to pray for you for three months prior, and Lois's turned out to be the Tollefsons, people she had never liked. To think that every night over supper Val Tollefson had bowed his big thick head and said, "And, Lord, we ask thee to strengthen Lois in her faith"—the same man who said once, "You won't amount to a hill of beans. You don't have the sense that God gave geese." She could feel her faith slip a little. She felt guilty, because Dave wasn't supposed to be there, and she was supposed to be ironing her confirmation dress, but he had walked two miles from his house, so what could she do? She felt sorry for Dave. He always has a bad haircut and a swarm of pimples on his forehead, but she likes him—he's quiet and nice. They talked to each other at Luther League get-togethers about what it would be like to be someone else, someone famous, for example, like Willie Nelson—you could use your fame to do good—and they went for one walk halfway around the lake, holding hands, and then she got the long letter saying how much she meant to him, twenty-seven pages, which was much more than she wanted to mean to him; it scared her.

She didn't know that Dave was a born writer. That twenty-seven pages is nothing to him; he did thirty-one on the death of his dog, Buff. She told him it would be better if they didn't see each other anymore. Friday night he walked over, full of more to say. She had four little brothers and a sister to take care of, so he sat on the old red sofa with a bottle of orange pop and watched as she fed the baby, and she turned on the TV and lost her faith. Men in khaki suits were beating people senseless, shooting them with machine guns, throwing the bodies out of helicopters. The reception was so poor, the picture so fuzzy, it was more like radio, which made the horrors worse, and she thought, *This could happen here.* It gave her a cold chill to imagine violent strange men busting in, as they had done to Anne Frank. She held the baby, Karen, imagining all of them were hiding from Nazis, and heard twigs crunch outside and knew that this boy could not protect her. She prayed and heard something like an echo, as if the prayer was only in her head. The whole world in the control of dark powers, working senseless evil on our lives, and prayer went no place. Prayer just went up the chimney like smoke.

When Marilyn cut the confirmation cake and served it with butter brickle ice cream, Lois thought, *I should say something. Like "I don't believe in God, I don't think."* Nobody would need coffee then.

After dinner she put on her jeans and a white jacket and walked out across the cornfield toward the road and the ravine to think about her faith on this cloudy day, and walking west over a little rise, she saw, just beyond the ravine, a white car she'd never seen before, and a strange man in a trench coat standing beside it. She walked toward him, thinking of the parable of the Good Samaritan, thinking that perhaps God was calling her to go witness to him and thereby recover her faith. He stood and pitched stones up over the trees, and as she got closer, he turned and smiled, put out his hand, and came toward her. She saw her mistake. Something glittered in his mouth. She stopped. He was a killer come looking for someone; it didn't matter to him who it was—anyone who came down the road would do. He walked toward her; she turned and fell down and said, "Oh, please, no. Please, God, no."

I hadn't seen her for five years. I said, "Lois, Lois—it's me." I helped her up. "How are you? It's good to see you again." We shuffled along the rim of the ravine, looking for the thin path down, and she told me about her confirmation, which I have an interest in because I am her godfather. I wasn't invited to church, I reckon, because fourteen years ago I wasn't anyone's first choice for godfather. I was nominated by Marilyn because Daryl suggested his brother Gunnar and she thought that was ridiculous, and to show Daryl what a poor choice he would be, she suggested me, and Daryl said, "Sure, fine, if that's what you want," and they were stuck with me.

The baby was named for her mother's Sunday school teacher, who was my Aunt Lois, my youngest aunt, so young she was like an older sister. She was single when I was a boy and so had plenty of time for her favorite nephew. She told me I was. She said, "Don't tell the others, but you are the one I love more than anyone else," or words to that effect. We were riding the bus to Minneapolis, she and I, to visit Great-Aunt Posie. Lois seemed young to me because she loved to pretend. We imagined the bus was our private bus and we could go anywhere we wanted. We were *somebody*.

My favorite game was Strangers, pretending we didn't know each other. I'd get up and walk to the back of the bus and turn around and come back to the seat and say, "Do you mind if I sit here?"

And she said, "No, I don't mind," and I'd sit. And she'd say, "A very pleasant day, isn't it?"

We didn't speak this way in our family, but she and I were strangers, and so we could talk as we pleased.

"Are you going all the way to Minneapolis, then?"

"As a matter of fact, ma'am, I'm going to New York City. I'm in a very successful hit play on Broadway, and I came back out here to Minnesota because my sweet old aunt died, and I'm going back to Broadway now on the evening plane. Then next week I go to Paris, France, where I currently reside on the Champs-Elysées. My name is Tom Flambeau—perhaps you've read about me."

"No, I never heard of you in my life, but I'm very sorry to hear about your aunt. She must have been a wonderful person."

"Oh, she was pretty old. She was all right, I guess."

"Are you very close to your family, then?"

"No, not really. I'm adopted, you see. My real parents were Broadway actors—they sent me out to the farm thinking I'd get more to eat, but I don't think that people out here understand people like me."

She looked away from me. She looked out the window a long time. I'd hurt her feelings. Minutes passed. But I didn't know her. Then I said, "Talk to me. Please."

She said, "Sir, if you bother me any more, I'll have the driver throw you off this bus."

"Say that you know me. Please."

And when I couldn't bear it one more second, she touched me and I was myself again.

And the next time we rode the bus, I said, "Let's pretend we don't know each other."

She said, "No, you get too scared."

"I won't this time." I got up and came back and said, "It's a very pleasant day, isn't it? Are you going to Minneapolis?"

Eventually we do. We pretend to be someone else and need them to say they know us, but one day we become that person and they simply don't know us. From that there is no bus back that I know of.

Lois Tollerud asked me, "Why did you stop here?"

I told her I had parked by the ravine, looking for a spot where our Boy Scout troop used to camp and where Einar Tingvold the scout-master got so mad at us once, he threw two dozen eggs one by one into the woods. Each egg made him madder and he threw it farther. When he ran out of eggs, he reached for something else. It was his binoculars. He didn't want to throw them away, but he was so furious he couldn't stop—he threw the binoculars and reached for them in the same motion. Heaved them and tried to grab the strap as they went by. We scouts looked for them for a whole afternoon, thirty years ago. Whenever I go by the ravine, I look for a reflection of glass, thinking that if I found those binoculars by some wonderful luck and took them back to him, he might forgive me.

"That's not true, is it?" she said.

"No, it's not." I stopped there because, frankly, I'd had a lot of coffee, but I couldn't tell her that. We walked for almost a mile along that ravine, to the lake and back, and then I felt like I'd like to visit her family after all.

We walked in. I got a fairly warm hello and was offered coffee. "In a minute," I said. "Excuse me, I'll be right back." I had a cup and a slice of cake that said "con but for," a little triangle out of her verse.

*Be not conformed to this world: but be ye transformed.* Our lovely world has the power to make us brave. A person wants to be someone else and gets scared and needs to be known, but we ride so far on that bus, we become the stranger. Nevertheless, these things stay the same: the sweet breath, the rain, the tendre croppes, and the smale foweles maken melodye—God watches each one and knows when it falls, and so much more does he watch us all.

*He honored what he knew to be right by remaining faithful to it.*

21

# Memorial Day

It has been a quiet week in Lake Wobegon, my hometown. It's been warm and pleasant, and many people put their boats in on Memorial Day weekend, including Clarence Bunsen, who has an orange sofa bolted to the bottom of his, and around the hull, just under the gunwales, painted in black letters: "O blessed mood, in which the burden of the mystery, in which the heavy and the weary weight of all this unintelligible world, is lightened." A saying that he found on a men's clothing calendar. He likes to lie out there on the water and meditate, and the fish don't bother him at all except the occasional one who needs help getting off the hook.

It is the beginning of summer, Memorial Day, which in some places is known as Decoration Day, and there are parades of interior decorators holding up wallpaper samples and swatches of drapes. But in Lake Wobegon, it is the day to honor our dead.

Monday, everyone who was not on the verge of death himself trudged up the hill to the cemetery for Memorial Day, and of course it was late getting started, so we walked around and looked at graves. There is the grave marker for the four teenagers killed in that terrible car crash in the spring of 1955, which none of us who were alive then will forget. The memory of them is reawakened every spring. There is the mysterious marker for Mamie Buehler, who lived alone in a stucco house on a large lot on the edge of town, a recluse who tended her apple trees and her garden, and you could hear her talking to herself in a quiet voice. The ladies of the Lutheran church did her shopping for her, and they said she kept up a conversation all day. Many people had never seen her, though she lived there all her life. And she was buried under a stone that said "Mamie Buehler" on one side and "Margaret Sullivan" on the other. After she died, there were rumors of an illegitimate daughter, perhaps, but no Margaret Sullivan has shown up, and now people think that when Mamie died, so did Margaret. That Margaret was the person Mamie talked to all those years.

It's quite an accomplishment, in a town where there are no secrets from anyone, for Mamie to have kept this large a secret all her life. We admire her more and more as years go by.

And finally the honor guard came marching up the road and we stood and sang "America the Beautiful" with the Ladies' Sextet leading and the rest of us trying to drown them out. There are seven of them, and they sing with a great deal of confidence. Why compound lack of talent with modesty?

We sang "Rock of Ages, Cleft for Me," and I was standing on the corner on one cold and cloudy day when I saw the hearse come rolling, come to carry my mother away, and Mr. Berge recited:

In Flanders fields the poppies blow
Between the crosses, row on row,
That mark our place; and in the sky
The larks, still bravely singing, fly
Scarce heard amid the guns below.

And then he wiped his eyes and said:

Breathes there the man with soul so dead
Who never to himself hath said,
"This is my own, my native land!"
Whose heart hath ne'er within him burned
As home his footsteps he hath turned
From wand'ring on some foreign strand?

They did not do the Gettysburg Address this year, and when we came to the place in the program where it usually goes and it wasn't there, it was like a death in the family. Nobody had decided to leave it out, but the sixth-grade teacher whose students would have recited the address had been expecting someone to send her a memo, and nobody did—because of course there are no memos about Memorial Day; we just go up there and do it. It's our obligation to the dead to remember them, and Lincoln said this in such a succinct and decent way that of course we would want to use his words.

Pastor Ingqvist gave the speech, which was brief. He said we should be grateful for the guidance given us by our elders and hope that we could offer something as good to our own children and be as good examples to them, and he mentioned his uncle Mr. Enger as having been a good example. His uncle was a man of simple faith who arranged his every day so that he arose early, feeling well rested, and sat in a chair and prayed and read his chapter of Scripture, and he did this first no matter what other pressing business he had. He honored what he knew to be right by remaining faithful to it. And on Memorial Day, we honor others who did likewise. Some of them did their service by counting sheets and towels or boiling potatoes, and others carried loaded weapons up a hill into the smoke, but all of them shared one code of honor: that they would, for the sake of the others, go into the smoke with them.

It was a good speech, and it should be given, though I wish that one Memorial Day someone would stand over the graves of the honored dead and talk about arrogant and deceitful old men who, to save their own asses, sent young men to die in battles that had no purpose and wars that should not have been fought except that nobody dared to say so at the time.

I remember Mr. Enger as the Memorial Day speaker when I was in sixth grade, and he stood up next to the dark angel on the pedestal, the monument to the Grand Army of the Republic, and he was holding a sheaf of papers, and I remember the cold horror that ran through the crowd when we realized that he was intending to read each and every page.

Mr. Enger was the last person you'd expect to give a speech. He was a man who'd panic if you asked him for the time of day. He was a farmer, and speaking was not part of his life, and he gave the speech,

I think, because he was trying to reform and not be so timid and to put himself forward, and so he stood up and bravely read a long and badly written speech in a voice that was practically inaudible for about twenty minutes, and he did not seem to be aware of us—he was doing the speech as he would have plowed a field, up and back and up and back—and some people in back managed to crawl over the hill and escape, and we could hear them laughing as they walked down to the town, and the poor Sons of Knute honor guard stood swaying in the sun, and the Ladies' Sextet had the facial expressions of demented ax murderers, and the sixth-grade students standing in rows were at the ends of their ropes, and finally Mrs. Enger got up the courage to walk over and whisper to him, and he looked up and said, "My wife tells me that some of you have dinner in the oven, and so the remainder of the speech will be at my house if anyone should wish to read it. Thank you very much." This was the year that they forgot to put blanks in the honor guard's rifles, so when they fired the salute, several chickadees fell out of the tree they aimed at, which was also the tree that the boy who played taps sat in. He did not fall out, but when he played taps, it was shakier than usual and the high note was a half-step high—it was like the cry of a carnivorous bird.

And everyone left as fast as possible and went home and put lighter fluid on the coals and sliced the buns and made the patties. One of the best parts of Memorial Day is when it's over, and having glanced at death, you can now make lunch and talk to people, and everything is more vivid and pleasurable for having gone up the hill.

When I was young, the cemetery was the only place in town where you could go with your friends at night and be alone and talk and not be overheard and stay out as late as you like; nobody would bother you up there. Some of us liked to go up there and take a flashlight and set it in the grass and sit around it and talk, and much of it was silly, kids trying to scare each other, boys lighting gas or talking about it, and a lot of it was young kids striking a pose and tossing off a piece of dialogue, kids acting, but so much of it was truly memorable. I remember the eagerness, the leaning forward, the excitement of ordinary pleasures—the pleasure of sitting in the dark and talking about the future, the summer ahead, the next school year, the distant future when you would do something—be something—something would be expected of you—you would teach, or work in an office, or work at something—but that was far off. It was too far away to be real to us. We were not planners; we were romantics. We lay on our backs in the cemetery and looked up at the stars, and someone reached over and turned off the flashlight, and the sight of the Milky Way was so intense to me, I almost lost track of the force of gravity and felt that I was standing with my back to a grassy precipice and in front of me yawned a vast darkness broken by brilliant light and behind me in the ground were our dead, who now had ventured out into that dark, and I felt that I would cling to the precipice as long as possible and then I would walk out and join them. A terrifying and exhilarating thought. And everything about this grassy precipice seemed precious, our shoes, our ice cream, our beds, the immense oaks, the smell of new mown grass and fresh asphalt, and I felt like one of those tenacious plants that puts down roots and will never give up, that wants to live. And then we got up and walked home.

*O blessed mood, in which the burden of the mystery, in which the heavy and the weary weight of all this unintelligible world, is lightened.*

*Why blame people who failed? All you do is encourage young people to imagine they can learn to avoid mistakes, and that's crazy— life happens to everybody, so why shouldn't there be an event where people who believe in monogamy honor those who tried and went down?*

# 22

# Marital Memorial Day

It's been cool this week, cool enough that you went to bed some nights worried about frost, and the crops are slow getting started but there's some green showing out in the fields, and some people are even starting to harvest the first rhubarb, and rhubarb, as you know, is a key ingredient in the good life, so things are moving, and as for frost, there comes a time when you have to stop worrying about it. Winter is a great season that teaches us powerful lessons, but school is out now—it's May, time to move on and study something new.

The last couple of weeks, Lake Wobegon has become a battleground in what seems like a civil war between nations of raccoons, and just about everyone in town has been awakened late at night by bloodthirsty shrieks and screams—including Gary and LeRoy, the town constables, called out in the middle of the night three nights in a row by Hjalmar Ingqvist, who thought it was burglars breaking in. One theory is that the raccoons have over-bred and this causes territorial squabbles and we are sort of the Gettysburg in this saga, and the other theory is that there's no battle at all—it's simply mating season—but if this is raccoon marriage we're hearing out there in the night, you wish they'd keep it to themselves as we do.

The cries in the night seem so human, especially when you sit bolt upright out of a deep sleep and hear this piercing scream from right under your open window. Or if, just as you awaken, your spouse does, too, and reaches over and grabs you, say, by the throat. Accidentally. But still, it's your throat. Clarence Bunsen almost levitated right out of the bed. He told Arlene, when they both started breathing regularly again, that he was glad they'd never kept loaded weapons within reach, or they might both be dead. One advantage of living in a peaceful town is there's more latitude for panic; in a big city, you have to keep calm at all times, otherwise you could get into trouble. This tends to compress human behavior.

Arlene and Clarence debated the raccoon problem in the morning over their breakfast—Clarence upholding the territorial warfare theory, Arlene saying they were just mating—and then Arlene looked up over her coffee and said, "You know, there ought to be a Memorial Day for marriages."

"A what?" he said.

"A Memorial Day when we honor those who have been divorced. Our noble fallen."

"Well," he said, "I can think of a few divorced people I wouldn't care to honor."

"Oh," she said, "there were plenty of men who got killed in wars who probably had it coming to them, too, but that's not the point. Marriage is noble. It's admirable and brave and very idealistic for anyone to ever imagine they could live with another person all their life—it's much nobler than going to war and more dangerous—and in the course of things some marriages crash, and others, like ours, pull through, and you know it could've been us just as well as them, so why blame people who failed? All you do is encourage young people to imagine they can learn to avoid mistakes, and that's crazy—life happens to everybody, so why shouldn't there be an event where people who believe in monogamy honor those who tried and went down?"

"Where are you going to hold this?" he asked. "At church?"

She looked at him coolly. "Of course. That's where they got the idea to get married in the first place. Of course it should be in church. Why not?"

They hadn't gotten much sleep that night, so they took naps that day, and she didn't mention the Marital Memorial Day idea to him again, but he thought about it. He thought, *This could be the idea that, if I brought it up at a church board meeting, would cause them to thank me for my many years of service and I wouldn't have to fund-raise anymore.*

He thought of it again a week ago Thursday morning when he was in Ralph's Pretty Good Grocery, looking over the selection of breakfast cereals, comparing the various claims as to fiber and naturalness, shopping for eternal life, and from the other side of the cereal, he heard a man say, "Well, what kind did you get? The most expensive, I suppose. Give me that."

A woman whispered, "Please. Don't."

He said, "Look at this. Look at this. Where am I supposed to get the money to pay for that? Huh? Tell me that. What are you crying for?" And then the woman put the can back on the shelf and went out the front door.

Clarence looked toward the front and his eyes met Judy Ingqvist's— she had heard, too—and then Clarence's eyes filled with tears. He had heard this argument before, and it affects him more than raccoons do, because he heard it when he was little. His father, coming home from the garage in 1934, deep in debt, too many kids, no hope on the horizon, and he'd see a can of tuna on the counter and all his anger would come out. He'd had to be nice to customers all day, and his tremendous Norwegian sense of formality wouldn't allow him to go get drunk in the bar and get in a fight and roll around on the floor and work it out that way—no, he could only come home to the one he loved and see that she'd paid sixteen cents more for something than he thought she should've and out it all came. How shameful, to argue about money. How small and mean. There is no meanness like marriage on its sour days—those little grinding arguments that can go on for weeks and eat up all of your goodwill and all your sense of humor if you let them. Clarence put the cereal back. He bought a jar of instant coffee. He left and walked to the garage, full of sadness, thinking of his father.

Judy Ingqvist left and went home full of purpose and with an armload of groceries. She walked into the house and into the pastor's study, and there was David, reading, and she told him she'd seen Chuck and Jennifer Rasmussen fighting and she said, "This parish is not doing enough for families under stress. You stand up there week after week and preach to the same comfortable, well-fed Lutherans, and it's time you let the less fortunate among us know that the gospel is for them, too. A young couple from this church should not feel so alone in the world that they have to stand in the grocery store and argue about paying twenty-nine cents more for a can of soup."

So he took it up in the sermon last Sunday. He spoke of Jesus' promise never to leave us alone and said that this promise is for us to carry out for each other. He said, "No marriage stands alone; no family can stand alone. A child cannot be raised properly by only two parents acting alone. A child needs at least two parents and aunts and uncles and grandparents and a church and a school and a community, and those two parents need the support and love and—if necessary—the practical help, the monetary help, of their fellow Christians." It was a good sermon, one that made the Republicans in the church restless, and as he gave it, he looked toward Chuck and Jennifer Rasmussen in the fourth row. He looked at them in what he thought was a warm, caring way, but he does have a stern face, and evidently he scared them, because they didn't come out the front door for the pastoral handshake after the service. He peered back in the door and thought he saw them slink toward the rear exit, and he said, "Excuse me, be right back," to Val Tollefson, a Republican who was about to shake his hand, and he ran around back, and sure enough, the Rasmussens were just getting into their car, and he dashed up and said, "Chuck, Jennifer, I just want you to know that whatever your needs are, this church and this pastor are ready to help, anytime, no questions asked."

"That's nice," they said, "but we're not Chuck and Jennifer. We're Doug and Karen. The Ericksons. You married us eight years ago. Remember?"

"Doug. Karen. Of course. How are you?" he said. "But the same goes for you, too. Anytime. No questions asked."

He walked back to the front door. Val Tollefson was there. "Interesting sermon," he said. "Kept me awake anyway. But then, so do the raccoons."

Pastor Ingqvist felt low all day. He tried to call the Rasmussens, but they weren't home. He kept trying, and then a woman answered who said they'd moved two years ago. Evidently they hadn't filled out a pew card for a while. He imagined them, a young couple slowly being overwhelmed by things, feeling angry and ashamed, getting more and more isolated from the church they'd grown up in, and the church becoming more and more a citadel of the smug and the lucky, and after thinking about this on Monday and feeling good and guilty about it, on Monday night Pastor Ingqvist went to the Sidetrack Tap and spent a couple of hours there. He went back on Tuesday and Wednesday. Lutheran ministers do not do these things by halves. He felt that if Jesus were in this town, that is where Jesus would go and be among sinners and drunkards. He wasn't sure if Jesus would have had a couple of bottles of Wendy's beer, or if Jesus would have had a Perrier. Or if Jesus would've ordered a Perrier and turned it into a Wendy's.

The clientele of the Sidetrack Tap is a mellow bunch in the evening. They've seen people with green hair come in, people with leather jackets and bike chains, people waving pistols, women with their skirts up over their heads, so a Lutheran minister throws no fear into their hearts. Just another wayfarer to them. He tried to fit in. Put a couple of quarters in the jukebox, tried to pick a few songs that seemed from the titles not to be blasphemous and to give a positive message about love—not easy to find. He sipped his beer, he glanced at the ball game, he commiserated with Wally about Wally's motor home and what a lemon that's been. Wally and Evelyn were planning to retire in that thing and tour the country, and instead he's going to have to work his tail off to pay the repairs. And after he said, "work my tail off," he looked at Pastor Ingqvist and said, "Pardon my French."

The pastor wondered, *Am I so pious looking that people have to apologize to me for vulgarity as mild as that?* So he told Wally the joke about Balaam's ass. "Who was the most elastic man in the Bible?" he said.

"I dunno," said Wally.

"Balaam, because he tied his ass to a tree and walked for twenty miles."

Wally did not get it. He had to explain to him that Balaam is a man in the Bible.

"Oh, I see," said Wally.

So he told a couple of Ole and Lena jokes, those great monuments to Norwegian vulgarity. He told the one about Ole coming home with Sven and yelling, "Hey, Lena, get us a beer. I brought Sven," but Lena was making love to another man—Ole walked through the living room and into the kitchen, Sven behind him, and Ole got out a couple of beers and gave one to Sven. "Here," he said. Sven said, "What about that man making love to Lena?" Ole said, "Tellwithim, he can get his own beer."

"Ja," said Wally. "That's a good one."

How ridiculous to sit there telling old jokes to a bartender. He knows them all.

Pastor Ingqvist skipped Thursday—too much smoke—and was thinking about going back Friday, but he got busy, and now he's thinking he'll go back Monday, but meanwhile he got a friendly call from the bishop. "Danny," said the bishop, "just calling to see how you are."

"It's David," said Pastor Ingqvist. "David."

"David, just calling to see how things are going. I've been concerned about you, David. David, sometimes I don't think we do a very good job about supporting our own clergy when they run into a rough stretch—I mean, gosh, we're out there trying to save the world and we forget about the laborer—and I just want you to know that I'm available anytime. Anything you want to take up with me, personal things, I don't care what, I want you to bring in without—David, I don't want you to be afraid to come in with your problems, that's all I wanted to say."

Pastor Ingqvist said, "That's good. I appreciate that," but he thought, *Informers in this town, watching the bars, mean-spirited small-town Lutherans, trying to get my ass in hot water—nothing ever changes. You can preach the gospel all your life, and it never sinks in; it's like planting flowers on Formica. God help you. In some ways,* he thought, *I would rather be a minister to the raccoons.*

## 23

# An Outdoor Reception by the Lake

t has been a quiet week in Lake Wobegon. A week of spectacular thunderstorms, the Lord trying to get the attention of his rather phlegmatic people. Midsummer is not far away, when the days start getting shorter again. Flag Day was the fourteenth, and there were flags flying from the light poles downtown and little flags stuck in the boulevards and people flying flags from their front porches. Flag Day is one of those arbitrary days—Why do we have Flag Day? To honor the flag. Why do we honor it? Because we do. But why on June 14? Because that's Flag Day. And it's good for children to learn about arbitrariness because you find a lot more of it as you get older.

The radishes and lettuce and spinach are coming in from the garden, and the tomatoes should be ready in a few weeks. Irene Bunsen, who prides herself on always having the earliest and the biggest and the tastiest tomatoes, woke up at two in the morning during a thunderstorm and heard hail on the roof, and she rolled her husband out of bed and tore the sheets off and dashed outside and covered her tomatoes and stood there, hailstones raining down on her, to make sure the sheets didn't blow off. Her nightgown was soaked and clung to her body, which in her case is not such a good idea, and there she was, light from the alley shining down, in full public view, looking like the captain's daughter tied to the mast of the wreck of the *Hesperus*, but the tomatoes were saved.

With all the rain we've had, the ground is soaked and the creeks are high and the lawns are like a wet sponge and the gardeners are owly about everything being behind and the farmers are worried: the soy-beans are in, but they need hot weather to get growing; very little corn is planted, and some people have given up on corn entirely. Mr. Hansen's eighty where he was going to plant corn is still too wet. So he's taken a job in St. Cloud as a van driver. He drives a fifteen-passenger van to the Minneapolis airport and back, three round-trips a day, men in dark suits talking on cell phones, all of them younger than he: fifteen men sometimes ratcheting away on their phones simultaneously—they sound like goats being herded into trucks. A few of them tip and most of them don't. One of the van drivers gets a lot of tips. For one thing, he's black, so tipping becomes an act of justice and a show of brotherhood. For another, he stands beside the van and helps the men out and looks them in the eye and says, "You have yourself a real good day now, and you come back and see us again real soon." That's tipping talk. Mr. Hansen doesn't even get out of the van. He just pulls up to the curb and says, "Well—looks like we made it." He could use the tips. But he can't see helping men out of a van or wishing them a good day. He's a farmer. Farmers talk by standing with their hands in their pockets and looking at the ground and saying, "Yessir. Yeah."

His daughter got married last week. It was expensive. My gosh, it was expensive. She married a boy named Lyle Peterson. Lorrie Hansen and Lyle Peterson, joined in rites of holy matrimony on Wednesday during a major thunderstorm, and Mrs. Hansen, in a moment of romantic fantasy, having seen this in a magazine, decided to have an outdoor reception by the lake, and they shelled out a lot of money to have it catered. Mr. Hansen sat up late one night thinking about it—"Ground wet, corn lost, no money coming in, and yet we have to throw all this money away on champagne and shrimp cocktail—I don't even like shrimp—and this liver pâté and Cajun pork morsels—we're not Cajun—what's the deal? Why not just have a ceremony in the living room and give all the money to the kids that you would've spent—why all this waste and expense?" Because. It's like Flag Day. It's how your wife wants it, because if it weren't done that way, she'd feel mean and miserly and she'd be afraid that some horrible thing would happen. The fatted calf must be killed.

Pastor Ingqvist has had three weddings this month, and there are four more to go. A busy time for him, especially since he insists on counseling the couple beforehand, and counseling Minnesotans is a slow process, like quarrying granite with a hammer and chisel. You do it an inch at a time. We are not a confessional people. Some people walk into the therapist's office and throw themselves down on the couch and can't wait to get started. Not us. We weren't brought up to talk about ourselves and our feelings, and when Pastor Ingqvist sits the young couple-to-be down in his office and tries to relax them with small talk (How's everything going? You both been well? Good. How's your folks? Good. Lot of rain we've been having), it only gets them both tremendously uptight. And then he leans forward and says, "I'd like to talk about how each of you feels when you're together, just the two of you—the good feelings and the not-so-good feelings, the doubts, the fears—and I'd like you to be completely honest with me and with each other. How about we start with you, Lorrie?" The mention of "not-so-good feelings" and of course the reference to honesty drives us Minnesota Lutherans right up the wall. Honesty. Fine. Go right ahead. Why don't we start with you, Pastor? How's everything between you and the missus? Be honest. Be my guest. But what if we all did it?

The honest truth is that most of these young people marry because they desperately want to have sex and be normal nice people, and it's impossible to do both in a small town without marrying someone, so two people sense each other's interest and availability, and powerful forces come into play, lust and the longing to be normal—and the mothers of the two of them exert their influence. A candidate is brought in for inspection and goes home, and afterward the mother says, "Well, I thought he was nice." And the way she says "I thought he was nice" communicates the fact that the boy is a dolt, about as bright as a mud fence, and none of this has much to do with honesty. It's more about sheer hope—that if you love somebody, or try to, and try to do the right thing, somehow it'll all work out over the long haul. And you set out down the highway of marriage, trying to ignore the many vehicles you see overturned in the ditch. And when the minister asks you your true feelings, you wonder, "Which ones? I have hundreds, many of them conflicting. Which ones you want to know about?"

Lyle Peterson and Lorrie Hansen were the quietest couple he'd ever counseled. They revealed nothing. Lyle remained silent, giving only his name, rank, and serial number. Lorrie never responded with more than three words, and often with two.

Mrs. Hansen got a job, too. She already had one, as a home care assistant, visiting old geezers and making sure they're taking their meds and bathing and eating, and then she got a weekend job at the ballpark taking the money and putting red dots on people's hands with a marker. It's a good job. Twenty-five dollars a game and all the cold or burned hot dogs you can eat—and it's sociable. The games of the Lake Wobegon Whippets are not so much about baseball as they are an all-purpose get-together. The game is to relieve us of the need for eye contact. People sit in the bleachers and talk about their kids, and the centerfielder, Ronnie Piggott, trots in and his mother stands up and yells, "I brought your laundry. It's in the trunk." Girls sit and look at the younger ballplayers and the way they flex and bend, which has less to do with baseball than with showing off the goods.

Mrs. Hansen stood last Sunday by the turnstiles and took money and made the red marks on people's hands, and suddenly she felt as if she were an angel at the gate, admitting people to the next part of their lives. All these young men in jean shorts and T-shirts with the sleeves cut off. The girls with their hair tied up and fashionably messy and dressed in tight and revealing string tank tops that are not a good idea if you're not a professional model and carrying a little extra. Would they have happy lives? Or did some tragedy await them? She wished they wouldn't be doing the expensive reception with the shrimp and champagne and the band and all, but she knew her husband would feel demeaned if they didn't. Would feel that his standing as a good provider would be called into question. If it were up to her, she'd just give the kids the money and wave them good-bye.

It was a nice wedding. The two nice people were joined in matrimony, and before having sex, they spent a few hours with their family and friends beside the lake, with the rain pouring down and the tables crowded in close under the tent and all the uncles and aunts and cousins and classmates there and people's hair stuck to their heads but the guests trying to eat and be merry but also trying to remember what they'd read about lightning strikes and large bodies of water as a jazz trio played valiantly. The lightning flashed nearby and the thunder crashed and the electric bass player stood perspiring, his eyes closed, and then the power went out and he became acoustic, and the coffee was cold, and the couple dashed away to Lyle's car and went off to do the forbidden thing, and the guests dashed for their cars, and only Mr. and Mrs. Hansen were left, sitting under the tent, him in a white tuxedo, her in a powder blue dress, listening to the band play "'Til There Was You," eating shrimp, of which there was a great deal left, and drinking champagne, which they're not used to, the rain pouring down, and somehow the extravagance started to make sense. A sort of Flag Day. Hard to explain. You have to live life; you can't just sit and think about how to. You have to jump in, and that's what arbitrary rules do—they make us jump. It's June and because your daughter wants to have sex and be a nice normal person, though you're losing your shirt, still you sit in a white tux under a tent eating shrimp and listening to a band and drinking champagne and starting to feel like Cary Grant. Hard to explain this, and thank goodness we are Lutherans and don't feel the need to say anything about it.

*I don't like to generalize about Lutherans, but one thing that's true*
*of every single last one of them without a single exception*
*is that the low point of their year is their summer vacation.*

# 24

# Lutheran Summer Vacation

It has been a quiet week in Lake Wobegon, my hometown. We've had beautiful weather, in the seventies, sunny, a little breeze. We've gotten plenty of rain, so the gardens are prospering. The Lake Wobegon Whippets lost last weekend to the Uppsala Uff-das. The Uff-das have one player whom all the Whippets hate—they call him Hammerhead—and he came up in the top of the ninth, with two out and the bases loaded, and he was swaggering and leering and smirking, and Ernie the old knuckleballer was mad and threw a hard one, high and inside, but when you throw the knuckleball hard, the ball doesn't hop and flutter—it's just a real slow fastball—and Hammerhead swung and hit a long, long, high fly ball deep to left center, and Ronnie in center and Fred in left both went hard for it, and you could see what was going to happen, two men dashing straight at each other, looking up into the sky, and the crack of their heads, you could hear it clearly in the bleachers, and down they went and the ball disappeared, and when the umpire got there, he found the ball in Ronnie's right pants pocket and called the batter out, and the Uff-das said he'd trapped the ball, and Ronnie wasn't saying anything—he thought it was Wednesday—but that was the call, he was out, and anyway, it wasn't important, since the Uff-das were leading 16–3 and won by the same score.

It was a sickening sound, those two heads cracking, and they both got headaches, but afterward in the Sidetrack Tap, Ronnie remembered all the words to "Today I Started Loving Her Again," which he used to know and hadn't sung in twenty years, and Fred remembered a passage from 1 Corinthians about faith, hope, and love that he'd learned as a child, so there did seem to be some good come of it. But then Fred remembered all sorts of other things he'd forgotten and he got quiet and moody, because it occurred to him that he had wasted his life and he was forty-two and he'd never get a chance to go back and do it right. They tried to cheer him up; they said, "Hey, you got a pickup and a camper, and it's all paid for, and you got a good secure job—you know, they're not laying off people in the cesspool pumping business—so you got work, and you got two nice kids you get to see on weekends, and you've got your own hair, and you haven't gained that much weight in the past couple of years. You really haven't."

To hear his friends describe his good luck depressed him so much that he walked out of the Sidetrack Tap and looked down at the beer bottle in his hand and threw it as hard as he could at his pickup truck and it hit the rear window of his camper and broke it. Gary and LeRoy were called to the scene, and he tried to get away, and there were sirens, and the next morning people asked each other what happened, and, well, it started with a guy named Hammerhead and a long fly ball to deep left center.

Here in the Midwest, we all have long memories of suffering and pain, because, for one thing, winter is so long, and when finally it gets warm and beautiful as it is now, finally—the last ice went out last week—we try to relieve these painful memories of cold, of neglect, of suspicion, darkness, anger, bologna sandwiches, stupidity, butterscotch pudding—we try to heal ourselves by subjecting ourselves to intensely pleasurable experiences—mindless pleasure in the sun while wearing as few clothes as possible—sand, air, water, sun, grass, gin— but we were not brought up to experience pleasure. It doesn't register on us. It's like trying to write on glass with a pencil. We get into as few clothes as possible and the sight of ourselves depresses us. Sunlight makes us gloomy. We are not Mediterranean people. We're Lutheran people. Even the Catholics up here are Lutheran. And I don't like to generalize about Lutherans, but one thing that's true of every single last one of them without a single exception is that the low point of their year is their summer vacation.

It's misery trying to decide where to go, because Lutherans are not brought up to express personal preference, and when you have two people saying to each other, "No, that's fine, if that's what you want, fine, that's okay, whatever, makes no never mind to me," often they compromise by going somewhere neither of them wants to go. Like the Happy Bison Motel in Bismarck, North Dakota. So there's dread and regret as the vacation approaches, and the Lutheran woman is thinking of various disasters that might befall them out there—psychotic hitchhikers, crazed bison, a berserk motel owner, a shower stall, you name it—and the Lutheran man is thinking, *I don't know how I'm going to pay for this with people leaving the lights on around here. You tell 'em and you tell 'em and you tell 'em and do they listen? No, they do not.* And they go to the Happy Bison Motel and it sits out on open grassland, a motel like a warehouse, surrounded by forty acres of asphalt, and there is a jungle gym and a wading pool and a cocktail lounge with a poker machine and a three-piece blues band called the Hitchhikers whom you can hear from anywhere in the motel until 3:00 a.m., and the trucks go by at 100 mph all night, and every night you dream about a different kind of death, and the air conditioner sounds like a power lathe, and your children come and sleep with you, and the phone rings at 6:00 a.m. and it's your sister—she's gone to check your house and the back door was unlocked and she found a half-eaten cheese sandwich on the kitchen table, and should she call the police? This is a Lutheran vacation. We endure it and we come back from it vowing to be better people.

Clarence and Arlene and Clint and Irene and the Knudsens are going to Norway in July. They're looking forward to that, though Arlene really wanted to see France—she's been to Norway twice—but she said, "No, that's fine. You want to go to Norway, we'll go." Clarence is not all that happy about spending two weeks with Irene, his sister-in-law, who since she stopped eating meat has been a different sort of person. A vegetarian way of life has opened her up to different levels of spiritual awareness that she can't help but want to tell people about, especially at mealtime. And the Knudsens are not easy. They're very nice, each one of them, but when you're with them, you notice that they never look at each other or address each other, and they refer to each other in the third person or by name, as if the other had died.

Wally and Evelyn are taking the motor home to the Grand Tetons. He has the idea that he'd like to videotape the entire route from Billings to Jackson Hole so he'll have this in future years. She wants to go to Las Vegas, but she's not going to mention it.

Father Wilmer is going canoeing on the St. Croix River with a band of priests he's been getting together with for seventeen years, called the Paddlin' Padres. They canoe and they camp and they eat simply and the money they save they spend on wine. Red wine. Montrachet and Pinot Noir and Cabernet and Châteauneuf-du-Pape, which is French for "Ninth House of the Pope," and they get good wine. Wine that costs twenty, thirty dollars a bottle. It's a sin, but it's only once a year. Last year they had a couple of forties and a sixty. This year Father Wilmer is bringing a $150 bottle of Chianti. A 1968. Priests in swimsuits lying on the river sand eating saltines and Swiss cheese and drinking $150 wine out of paper cups. Decadence their parishioners can hardly dream of.

David and Judy Ingqvist are going to spend most of August at her parents' cabin on Tremeleau Lake near Bemidji. He has to preach the last two Sundays at Lake Wobegon Lutheran, because his replacement, Pastor Ekerholm, could only come for three weeks. Pastor Ekerholm runs an outreach program in Minneapolis, and three sermons is all he has in his repertoire, one on stewardship and one entitled, "Taste Not the Unclean Thing," and the other is something about faith but mostly stories about golfing. The original deal was that they would get the parents' cabin to themselves, but Judy's brother Jack and his wife Cassandra decided to come up, too; their marriage is going through a lot of stress now what with Jack's drinking, so they thought it would be good to get away. Not what the Ingqvists had in mind, but Judy's mother begged them to please be nice to Jack and Cassandra. She said, "You know that Cassandra adores David. She just hangs on his every word. She'll listen to David."

Cassandra and Jack are the two unhappiest people David and Judy know, and they will now know them better. They are boring, unhappy people. They have slaved their lives away to have a beautiful home in the suburb of Eden Grove for the sake of their three children, and it is beautiful if grass is important to you, and their children grew up so afraid of the world outside of Eden Grove that they never had a desire to leave, but property values there are such that young people can't afford to buy homes on a checkout boy's salary, so they live at home with Jack and Cassandra. Three of them; the youngest is twenty-four.

Ralph is packing up his kids and going to Canada with Mrs. Ralph. They're taking the train north from Winnipeg up toward Churchill Bay, and it's a little train, four coaches and a mail car, that goes rattling along through the woods and stops whenever you pull the red cord. The train stops in the woods beside a river and four people get off with immense backpacks and disappear into the underbrush. Ralph and Mrs. Ralph are going to a lake they went to last year, called End of the Trail Lake. You need to take smoke bombs and about eight gallons of liquid detergent because the bugs there are so fierce that bug spray doesn't discourage them. They feast on Cutter's. But detergent seems to slow them down. A crucifix helps, but you have to hit them really hard. Ralph and Mrs. Ralph love to fish, and thanks to the bugs, that lake is magic for fishing. You put anything on the end of a line, a crouton and a piece of raw bacon and a copy of the *Reader's Digest*, and you throw it in and—bang—you've got a fourteen-pound walleye. Fishing takes up about two minutes of the day. You fish standing in the water up to your armpits because the bugs can't swim, and you smear the detergent in your hair and all over your arms and face, and you catch your fish and you clean the fish there in the water and you build a fire on top of sand piled on boards laid across an inner tube and you roast those fish out in deep water and eat them there. They're wonderful eating, though they taste slightly of detergent, and afterward you go to sleep in your tent or, on a hot night, on an air mattress, deflated so it'll lie low in the water. It's a vacation where after a week you know that you will never complain about anything that happens to you the rest of the year.

I broke off with the Sanctified Brethren to become a Lutheran, but as soon as I became a Lutheran, I started making fun of them so as to alienate them and make myself an outcast, which I'm much happier being.

# 25

# Potato Salad

It has been a quiet week in Lake Wobegon. It's been cool there and rainy and the sky turning dark and people tuning in their radios and hearing about "chance of severe thunderstorms with possible damaging winds, frequent cloud-to-ground lightning, and possible hail." There are dark Lutherans who enjoy the sense of impending doom. Some people wake up every morning thinking, *Chance of catastrophic illness with possibility of major surgery.* But some people don't bother with it. They just do what we did back in the old days when we didn't know any better. Just smell the air for rain and look at the clouds and decide whether to close the windows or not. Our descendants will probably carry weather radar on them, part of their PalmPilots, and whip it out when clouds appear. They'll be tracking storm cells for miles around. Being hit by lightning will be unheard of.

When I was a boy, there were numerous lightning victims, and we sort of knew who they were and we made allowances for them. Some woman who wore men's clothing and smoked a cigar and wore her hair short and liked to cut down trees, well, she'd been struck by lightning, you know. The old man who liked to go off in the woods for a few days and we were warned not to follow him, not to spy on him—you don't want to know—he'd been hit by a bolt of lightning. An electrical storm passed through, big thunderclouds like mountains rolling and rumbling and thunder like cannons and lightning ripping through the sky. A few weeks later you'd hear about somebody who had decided to ride a bicycle across the United States or write the Great American Novel or compose music based on the three tones that can be made by blowing across beer bottles or try to come up with the Unifying Theory of the Universe or make a midlife career switch and go into ballet—lightning.

They used to exhibit a man named Slocum at the county fair who had been struck seven times by lightning. He was a big man, slow afoot, and I imagine that being struck by ten thousand volts of electricity does not stimulate the intelligence. They said that he'd tried to get away from the first three or four strikes and then had resigned himself to his fate, and when a storm came up, he'd go stand in an open field with a fifteen-foot steel pole in his hands and a tin helmet, and then he came to believe it was his fate and he got to driving around in search of thunderstorms in a car with steel-belted tires and an extendable aerial he could raise eighty-five feet in the air, and he got his last two strikes that way. He sat in the tent at the fair in a white suit and Panama hat, and he was picking "Nearer, My God, to Thee" on a banjo as he whistled "Grandfather's Clock"—no easy thing—you get that from being struck by lightning. It was nothing you'd want to spend a whole afternoon watching somebody do, but it was interesting.

Our house was struck by lightning once on the Fourth of July. There was a storm and we paid little attention to it and then there was a crash like the sky had fallen, and for an instant there was a bluish light in the room, and everybody sitting eating fried chicken stood up and sang a high note—OOOOOOOOOOOOOOO—and then sat down, and nobody said a word about it afterward. If you mentioned it to any of them now, they'd all claim that I made it up, which is typical of my family. I remember it clearly: everyone standing, holding fried chicken, their hair sticking straight out, and singing OOOOOOOOOOOOOOO. And ever since then, we've been unable to speak any language but English. That's how deep an impression it made.

We always made a big thing of the Fourth of July in my family because we were brought up to believe that individuals are capable of intelligence and judgment but people get into groups and lose half their IQ and become susceptible to mania and delusion—Wall Street being a prime example, and then you have various religions whose theology no sensible child would accept for a minute, but here are armies of true believers willing to march to the Holy Land and capture Jerusalem in the name of it, or go to the mountaintop and await the Second Coming. There are the people who believe in magnetism and keep crystals in their pillows and attach electrodes to their temples to read their levels, and there's witch-hunting and book-burning and people who believe in the therapeutic value of various poisons, and all told, the great advances in learning come about by the diligent work of individuals, and the effect of groups is destructive. Think of the last committee you were part of—would you have entrusted that committee with the care of a small child? No. By the time that committee decided on the child's bedtime, the child would've grown up and left home. Committees are God's way of preventing change.

So our family celebrated a day in which one group of people split off from another group of people—it seemed like a happy thing to us—and we kept right on splitting off—we believed in the value of a good snit and walking out, slamming the door, and never speaking to those people again. Better yet, never speaking to them in the first place. We were Sanctified Brethren, we believed that God had bestowed his truth on us and on nobody else, and if our number had ever gotten above twelve, we'd have found some way to break off with the others and form a new and purer group. A new church of, say, three people. Two to procreate, and one to watch and make sure they didn't do it in an unscriptural way. I broke off with the Sanctified Brethren to become a Lutheran, but as soon as I became a Lutheran, I started making fun of them so as to alienate them and make myself an outcast, which I'm much happier being. Harmony makes me uneasy. That's why I'm a Democrat.

Enlightenment comes slowly, that's for sure, and some of us who may appear to be enlightened are actually no smarter than our ancestors. The apple didn't fall far from the tree. Every day around five or five-thirty, I have a strange restless feeling that it's time to do something. About the time other people are opening up the chilled white wine and getting out the shrimp cocktail and the Brie and the crackers, I have this empty, nagging, unhappy feeling, and it's simply because my dad's family had dairy cows and I'm old enough to remember and I still feel milking time coming on, and instead of getting the cows into the stanchions and wiping off their udders, I maybe rearrange the living room or get in the car and drive to the store and pick up six gallons of milk. I grew up tending a vegetable garden; now I'm an editor: similar work. Weeding and cultivating.

Planning committees are conferring for the family Fourth of July picnics and deciding who will make the fried chicken and who will make the pies, the tough ones, and who will make coleslaw or bring the pickles. Fried chicken is a true test of a cook—it's your senior term paper, the test that separates the summa cum laudes from the drones and the dullards. Anybody can slap ground beef on a grill, but to fry chicken so that the result honors that chicken's life and sacrifice is no easy thing. Some families just haul in a bucket of takeout, which is okay if you are giving a birthday party for a small child or for an elderly person with advanced dementia, but for the Fourth of July it seems sort of sad—to put this sodden, greasy, depressing food in front of those you love when with a little effort you could have produced something distinguished. What if Thomas Jefferson hadn't bothered to write the Declaration of Independence himself? What if he'd just downloaded a bunch of stuff he found doing a search on independence—actually it was about indolence and pendants, the kind that hang around your neck, but close enough, and he just slapped it together and they all signed it, John Hancock and Franklin and Washington and Madison and John Adams, and they said, "Let's go snarf up some greasy chicken and maybe buy a gallon of potato salad." It wouldn't have been the same country.

Potato salad. Don't get me started. People who are asked to bring potato salad to the picnic and instead stop at a convenience store and get some plastic tubs full of mushy potatoes, salad dressing, and mustard to give it that eerie yellow color. Why insult us? Do you think we've never had real potato salad and we can't tell the difference? Do you think we're not Americans and don't know potato salad? Do we look Canadian to you? Is there something Icelandic about us? Potato salad. No big mystery about it. It has hard-boiled eggs, fresh chopped celery, chives, green onions, real mayonnaise, maybe a little sour cream, plenty of dill, and on top you spread some sliced boiled eggs with a sprinkling of paprika. The great potato salad makers of the world are passing from the world, and you and I should emulate their art lest this country slide into barbarism and ignorance and decay. Standards must be upheld.

I didn't know I was going to write about potato salad; I was intending to write about independence. But when you get to my age, you take a shorter view because there's less up ahead. You may not believe in progress but you believe in people picking up after themselves and minding their manners and pulling their weight and showing kindness and attending to the details. Rewrite that page and make it better. Grow your garden. Teach your children.

Every child has the right to real potato salad and to hold a sparkler in his or her little hand and wave it around. What magic, to trace your little arc of light against the dark. Surely there have been thousands of men and women who gave their lives to art, to music, to the gaiety of language, who felt the first stirrings of artistry when they helped Grandma make a potato salad, a great potato salad that had texture, had some crunch, had the green onions working with the egg yolks and the paprika and dill and the richness of mayonnaise, which cries out for accompaniment with a fried drumstick, still warm with crackly skin and flaky meat. Oh, this is art, to take the humble potato and the stupid chicken and ennoble them with the craft of cooking—and is this not the meaning of our country, to take what is common and make something beautiful of it? To stand on the lawn in the twilight and wave your torch and draw big loops of light and slashes and make bold, brilliant strokes? Happy Fourth of July, everybody.

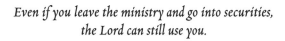

*Even if you leave the ministry and go into securities,*
*the Lord can still use you.*

# 26

# Raking Leaves

I t has been a quiet week in Lake Wobegon, my hometown. It was a beautiful, glorious week, fall in all its splendor, a splendor and a magnificence fit for kings and heroes and poets and bestowed on us humorists—glorious days that you walk out into, into the pageantry of trees, red and gold and blazing yellow and ochre, and the rich smell in the air, sweet and chill, brings everything back to you, your childhood, your aunts and uncles and the kids you ran around with on the playground and you fell in the cinders and went inside to wash off and you walked down the hall of the old school, the rooms empty, and you stepped into your classroom, all the desks empty, the autumn leaves pinned to the bulletin board, and your teacher's writing on the blackboard, the unit on verbs—he goes, she goes, they go, he went, she went, they went—and you thought, *I will always remember this, what it was like to be eight,* and after school you walked home past the old men who sat smoking on the bench in front of Ralph's and they stopped talking when you passed them by and you wondered, *What is the big secret?* And now you're older than those old men were and you stand on your front steps, these great moments, red and gold and yellow, the leaves are falling, and do you know what those old men knew? No, you don't. And soon all the leaves will be gone.

Pastor Ingqvist was raking leaves in the yard between his house and the church, wearing his old red plaid wool jacket and his brown hat that his wife gave him for his birthday. She said it made him look like a poet, like William Butler Yeats as a young man, and he's been wearing

159

it ever since—even though in this town, a great hat attracts comment. Men say, "Where'd you get the cowboy hat?" Though it isn't a cowboy hat; it's a poet's hat—it's an Irish poet's hat. "My wife gave it to me for my birthday." "Oh. Looks good on you. Now all you need is a horse to go with it." And they laugh, as if this were quite humorous, har de har har, and being the pastor, he is supposed to chuckle and grin at this imbecile and shake his head, as if to say, "What a keen wit you have, my good man!" What stupid things people say and expect you to laugh.

No, this is the hat of a poet. A poet like Yeats, who wrote:

The trees are in their autumn beauty,
The woodland paths are dry,
Under the October twilight the water
Mirrors a still sky;
Upon the brimming water among the stones
Are nine-and-fifty swans. . . .
Unwearied still, lover by lover,
They paddle in the cold
Companionable streams or climb the air;
Their hearts have not grown old;
Passion or conquest, wander where they will,
Attend upon them still.
But now they drift on the still water,
Mysterious, beautiful;
Among what rushes will they build,
By what lake's edge or pool
Delight men's eyes, when I awake some day
To find they have flown away?

He was raking the leaves and out of habit was raking the pile toward the curb, as if he were going to burn them in the street, the way we used to, instead of putting them into plastic bags, and he heard the phone ring in his office and he thought about going to answer it and then didn't and a moment later along came Eunice Ingqvist, his cousin Jack's wife, and she said, "David, can you do a baptism on Sunday? I know it's the last minute, but I'd really appreciate it—"

"Of course," he said. "Who?"

"My nephews," she said. "Nancy's boys. Down in the Cities. I don't know if she's going to allow this or not, and I probably won't know until Saturday night. Is that all right?"

"Of course," he said. "You bring 'em in and we'll baptize 'em."

Eunice was all bundled up. Eunice is a low-thermostat person. She believes in dressing warm and saving on fuel. Her husband, Jack, is a high-thermostat person. Eunice believes that heat makes people stupid. She sees evidence of this. The other day, he said, "What happened to that old motto we had hanging up over the breakfast table?"

She said, "The one your mother gave us? The needlepoint?"

"Yes."

"I threw that away about ten years ago."

"Oh. Why?"

"I was tired of looking at it."

"Oh."

It was a plaque with a picture of an owl, and underneath it said: "The wise old owl sat in the oak. The more he saw, the less he spoke. The less he spoke, the more he heard. Why can't we be like that wise old bird?"

Eunice decided that Norwegians have enough silence in them without trying for more. Urging a Norwegian man to be silent is like teaching a fish to swim.

He said, "Is it cold in here?"

"No," she said. "It's fine."

"It feels like it's about sixty degrees in here."

"It is sixty. Put on a sweater."

Pastor Ingqvist got his leaf pile together and went off to get the plastic bags. The ban on burning really killed off the pleasure of leaf raking. You raked them into the gutter and lit them and you stood there tending the fire. Watching the smoke rise. It felt like a man's work, a lonely, dignified job, the setter of fires, the sentry, the guardian, the watchman. Guys would come and stand around with you as you poked at the burning leaves in an expert way that guys know and got the fire to blaze up; they would stand around communicating in that silent way that guys have, and then the town council voted in this ban—which has to do with clean air, which of course you can't be against—and that's one of the problems with democracy. There are so many things you can't be against, so you have to go along with it, even though it's a terrible idea. The smoke drifting through town on an October evening, it made fall something sacred and mysterious and legendary—"This is the time of great smokes, my son; this is the time when the twilight is hazy with memory. Now we go to light the fires. As the ancient ones did, so do we now, my son." And then they voted it out. The fools. He'd love to light these leaves. He'd love to, so much. But he's the Lutheran pastor. It can't be done.

He stopped in his office and got the message from the answering machine. It was a man's voice. He didn't recognize it. The man said, "Pastor Ingqvist—? Well, that's all right, I'll call back. That's okay. I was just thinking maybe you'd be in. I was going to—uh—well, I'll call back. That's okay." Odd message. He played it over. It sounded like someone from around here, all right. But what did he want?

He came back to the leaves, carrying the plastic bags, and a strange man stood by them. He wore a tweed wool sport coat and a gray sweater under it and tan pants and loafers. Not from here. And he smoked a pipe. "David," he said. "Hi. It's Merle. Merle Sanderson. Remember?"

David didn't, but he's the Lutheran pastor; the pastor isn't supposed to not remember. David said, "Sure. How are you, Merle?"

"I'm fine. Just dropped by. I was heading up to Fargo to look at this Internet company up there, thought I'd stop in—it's been more than twenty years."

"Right," said David. "Well, you look good." Who was this person? Didn't look Lutheran at all.

"Kinda surprised to find you still here, actually."

"Yeah," David said. "Surprises me, too. Twenty-six years. Long time."

"Yeah," the man said. "I left the ministry after that pontoon boat sank. You remember that?"

And now it all came back. Merle Sanderson. He was a pastor at the church out west, Minneota, and he was one of the twenty-four Lutheran ministers who came to town on a fact-finding tour, and

Pastor Ingqvist was going to have a wiener roast for them, and then Wally at the Sidetrack offered the use of his pontoon boat, the *Agnes D.*, and Wally tossed in six cases of beer and the wieners and buns, and put the grill in the stern, and all the pastors trooped aboard—a painful memory. Pastor Ingqvist stood on the dock as they all boarded, and he could see the boat was overloaded, but he didn't want to be the one to say, "Some of you are going to have to get off." He was tempted to push the boat away from the dock and wave to them and say, "You have a good time and don't worry about me." But he climbed on, and as he did, he felt the deck tip and there was water in his shoe. Still, Wally gunned the engine and the boat pulled away, riding about a half inch above the water—oh, it was painful.

"Yeah," the man said. "I just didn't feel I was doing that much good, and I had three kids set to go off to college, and I went into the securities field and opened up my own firm and am doing very well. You invest much in stocks?"

No, David shook his head.

"This company in Fargo is good. Called Horseshit-dot-com. They sell horse manure to gardeners. People swear by the stuff. Honest. They get ten, fifteen bucks a pound for it. The stock has gone from four bucks a share to thirty-eight. It's hot."

David thought, *I oughta hit him up for a contribution.* Then he heard the phone ring. "Excuse me," he said. He dashed into the church. Into his office. It was Eunice calling. The baptism was on, she thought. And she wanted a full-fledged liturgical baptism, with sponsors and candles and everything. But would it be okay if the parents of the boys weren't there?

Eunice could smell fall in the air—the smell of apples and wood smoke and leather and horses—and it took her back to a day long ago when she was crossing the campus of the university, leaves crunching underfoot, on her way to meet the man she thought she was going to marry and did not. She was coming from a class on Yeats and was thinking of his poem, "Wine comes in at the mouth / And love comes in at the eye; / That's all we shall know for truth / Before we grow old and die. / I lift the glass to my mouth, / I look at you, and I sigh." He was a senior in journalism and the first man she really loved—real love, that flutter of excitement when you're on your way to meet, the trembling that never really goes away. She can still remember his smell, the feeling of him walking next to her, his arm around her waist.

Sometimes, when she isn't getting along with Jack, she imagines running into that man and him inviting her for a drink and her saying, "Well, sure." Sometimes, when she really isn't getting along with Jack, she imagines that she's a widow and that man comes from California to visit her for a weekend and he says, "Nice house," and she says, "Yes, I'm planning to sell it."

In the old days, the little group at the baptismal font was the young mother and father (Mr. and Mrs.) and another couple of similar age (also Mr. and Mrs.), and the men wore suits and the women wore dresses and the child wore a white baptismal dress. But now, all bets are off. The mother and father may have different last names, and are they married? Don't ask. Do they believe in the gospel of Jesus Christ and renounce the devil and all his pomps? Or do they simply believe that somewhere in the darkest night a candle glows and there is a divine spark that is within us all? Don't ask. Ours is not to reason why; ours is simply to baptize.

The grandparents sit in the front pew. Probably this was their idea. Probably Grandma said, "When are you going to have that child *baptized*, for heaven's sake?" And the young mother convinced the father to please show up at the church and wear something decent and don't invite your rock 'n' roll pals or I'll kill you and I mean it. And the child is anointed and tipped forward, and the water is applied in the name of the Father and the Son and the Holy Ghost, and then the minister holds the child in his arms and parades up the aisle with him and says, "Now I want to introduce to you the newest member of the family of God and Lake Wobegon Lutheran Church . . ." and every eye gleams, every member dabs at his or her eyes, there is applause.

This baptism was Eunice's idea. Her sister's boys are four and seven, and every week Eunice goes down to visit the three of them in their messy apartment so Nancy can go to her AA group. Nancy is forty-three and has had a lot of experiences that nobody else in the family has had, and she has a hard time talking to them. Like divorce. She divorced Bob, she told Eunice, because she just felt that the marriage wasn't growing anymore. Eunice looked around for the thermostat. Too warm in here. That's 75 degree thinking. Try 62 for a while.

Nancy is going to a church in Minneapolis, the sort of church where you don't necessarily have to believe in God and they don't call it a church—they call it a community of souls. Nancy's latest boyfriend is the janitor at the church; his name is Adam and he's fifty-six, twice divorced, in AA, and also in the Sons of Emotionally Distant Fathers Support Group. Eunice has met him once. A silent guy—what can you say? His hair is longer, he wears a Grateful Dead T-shirt, but it's the same silence. The temperature in this church, it's like a greenhouse. Nancy is taking her boys to this church where they don't have baptism, of course, but they do have a ceremony of Affirmation of Person-hood where everyone stands in a circle and holds hands and someone whangs on a little drum and bells are dinging and someone is playing a flute and the minister in her white caftan holds a candle and someone reads something from Whitman and there you are—welcome to the human race.

Eunice thought it'd be nice to put the water mark of the Lutheran church on these boys. They might grow up to be pagans but God could look down and see that water mark and say, "Well, okay, I guess. Maybe. We'll see."

Pastor Ingqvist told her to call him Saturday night if it was a go, and he went back out to the leaf pile.

Merle was there. "I gotta run," he said. "I'm late as it is. You ever hear from any of those other guys who were on the pontoon boat?"

"No, not really," David said.

"Just curious what happened to them."

David said good-bye and went back into his office. The sun was going down. Maybe the man who'd called him would try again now that it was suppertime. He could imagine a guy who was desperate and maybe hadn't been to church much in the past few years; maybe he was working Sunday mornings, and now the bank had told him they couldn't justify the loan based on what the government payment would be and the value of the land, so if he couldn't get the money, they'd foreclose. He used to deal with Cully at the bank, but now that bank's been bought by a big bank corporation in Minneapolis, which in turn is a subsidiary of one based in San Francisco, and when he talks to the bank, it's an 800 number and some very professional sympathetic voice gives him the bad news, and he just wants to say, "Who are you? Where are you? You've never even seen this farm."

The pastor sat in his dark office waiting for the phone to ring, imagining a desperate man sitting in the dark in his granary with a shotgun across his lap, listening to his wife call his name from the back door. "Call me," he said. "This time I'll be here. Call me. We'll call on the Lord. The Lord is an ever-present source of help in time of trouble. Call me. Don't hurt yourself. Don't do this. You'll hurt your wife and kids more than you can ever believe. They'd never get over it. Call me." And he could imagine holding the man in his arms, carrying him down the aisle of the church as the parishioners applauded.

And then he smelled smoke. Something was burning. He tore into the sanctuary. A little mist of smoke drifted through. He tore out the front door. The leaves were burning in the gutter. A long line of them. The smoke drifted up. A sign from the Lord. The smoke by day, the fire by night. Merle had knocked the ashes out of his pipe—that's probably what lit it—but it was still a sign from the Lord. Even if you leave the ministry and go into securities, the Lord can still use you. He stood by the leaves and breathed in the smoke and saw people looking out their windows at him. He didn't care. He stood and poked at it and got it burning hotter.

That's the news from Lake Wobegon, where all the women are strong, all the men are good looking, and all the children are above average.

*Believing there is always more than meets the eye*
*defeats the sense of sight.*

## 27

# Ninety-five Theses

A former Wobegonian wrote "Ninety-five Theses," a neatly typed manifesto that he brought home in late October 1980, along with a fine woman from Boston whom his parents wanted to meet, since he had married her a few weeks before. His parents live in a little white house on the corner of Branch and Taft, where his old bedroom under the eaves has been lovingly preserved. He left his wife to look at it and snuck away to the Lutheran church, intending to nail the "Ninety-five" to the door, a dramatic complaint against his upbringing, but then something in his upbringing made him afraid to pound holes in a good piece of wood, and he heard the Luther Leaguers inside at their Halloween pizza party and was afraid he would be seen—also, he was afraid the "Ninety-five" would blow away since all he had were small carpet tacks. So he took it downtown and slipped it under Harold Starr's door with a note that said, "Probably you won't dare publish this." Harold considered publication twice—first when his pipes froze and the office toilet burst, putting the Linotype out of commission and leaving him short of copy, and again when he had three wisdom teeth pulled and sprained his ankle, which he had hooked around the pedestal of the dentist's chair, and had to use crutches for three days, during which he heard the same joke about those teeth having long roots more than thirty times—but he held off, and the "Ninety-five" remains on his desk, in a lower stratum of stuff under council minutes and soil conservation reports. In the same stack are some letters from the anonymous author asking for his manuscript back. Like so many writers of manifestos, he forgot to keep a copy, and over the years his letters have descended to a pitiful pleading tone quite unlike his original style.

"I simply can't understand despite repeated requests. . . . This is very important to me. . . . The ms. is *mine* and I need it *now* for a longer work I'm writing. . . . I know you are busy and please forgive me if I seem impatient, but I beg you to *please* attend to this small matter. I enclose a stamped self-addressed envelope."

Five such envelopes sit in the stack, with five addresses that show a trend toward the east and south, with one brief long jump to California. Three are plain manila envelopes; two are Federal Express. The manuscript of "Ninety-five" has sustained some coffee damage but is in good shape, except for three pages that are missing. "They are around here somewhere. I remember seeing them," says Harold, "and as soon as I get this desk straightened around and find the damn things, I'll send it all back to him. I'm just one person, you know. I'm not the U.S. Post Office."

Here, unabridged, is the document as Harold has it.

*Ninety-five Theses*

1. You have fed me wretched food, vegetables boiled to extinction, fistfuls of white sugar, slabs of fat, mucousy casseroles made with globs of cream of mushroom, until it's amazing my heart still beats. Food was not fuel but ballast; we ate and then we sank like rocks. Every Sunday, everyone got stoned on dinner except the women who cooked it and thereby lost their appetites—the rest of us did our duty and ate ourselves into a gaseous stupor and sat around in a trance and mumbled like a bunch of beef heads.

2. Every Advent, we entered the purgatory of lutefisk, a repulsive gelatinous fishlike dish that tasted of soap and gave off an odor that would gag a goat. We did this in honor of Norwegian ancestors, much as if the survivors of a famine might celebrate their deliverance by feasting on elm bark. I always felt the cold creeps as Advent approached, knowing that this dread delicacy would be put before me and I'd be told, "Just have a little." Eating "a little" was, like vomiting "a little," as bad as "a lot."

3.  You have subjected me to endless boring talk about weather, regularity, back problems, and whether something happened in 1938 or 1939, insisting that I sit quietly and listen to every word. "How's it going with you?" you said. "Oh, about the same," you replied. "Cold enough for you?" It was always cold, always about the same.

4.  You have taught me to worship a god who is like you, who shares your thinking exactly, who is going to slap me one if I don't straighten out fast. I am very uneasy every Sunday, which is cloudy and deathly still and filled with silent accusing whispers.

5.  You have taught me to feel shame and disgust about my own body, so that I am afraid to clear my throat or blow my nose. Even now I run water in the sink when I go to the bathroom. "Go to the bathroom" is a term you taught me to use.

6.  You have taught me the fear of becoming lost, which has killed the pleasure of curiosity and discovery. In strange cities, I memorize streets and always know exactly where I am. Amid scenes of great splendor, I review the route back to the hotel.

7.  You have taught me to fear strangers and their illicit designs, robbing me of easy companionship, making me a very suspicious friend. Even among those I know well, I continue to worry: What do they *really* mean by liking me?

8.  You have taught me to value a good night's sleep over all else, including adventures of love and friendship, and, even when the night is charged with magic, to be sure to get to bed. If God had not meant everyone to be in bed by ten-thirty, he would never have provided the ten o'clock newscast.

9.  You taught me to be nice, so that now I am so full of niceness, I have no sense of right and wrong, no outrage, no passion. "If you can't say something nice, don't say anything at all," you said, so I am very quiet, which most people think is politeness. I call it repression.

10. You taught me to worry about my face. The fear of acne, which will follow me to my grave, began when I was fourteen, a time of life when a person has no skin but is all raw flesh (skin-colored), and grew a crop of zits around my nose and learned various positions, sitting and standing, in which I could keep a hand to my face. They were triggered by fear. You said, "I'd like you to have a nice complexion for Dorothy and

Bob's wedding. They'll be taking pictures." So I wound up looking like a three-bean salad. I died inside to see myself in the mirror. Better that those blotches meant nose cancer; at least I could go to the hospital and get flowers. What I had, people don't send flowers for. When I was sixteen, I bought the first ski mask in town. "Why don't you smile more?" you said.

11. You taught me, "When the going gets tough, the tough get going," teaching me to plod forward in the face of certain doom.

12. You taught me to be competitive even in matters of faith, to take pride in the great privilege of having been born Lutheran, even at moments of contrition. Religious intolerance was part of our faith. We believed that Catholics were illiterate peasants, foreign-born, who worshipped idols. In Sunday school, we looked up to see a gory picture of "Christian Infants Martyred at the Hands of Papist Clergy." We believed there was a secret tunnel between rectory and nunnery. We believed they poisoned the pets of Protestants. Whatever they believed, it wasn't right.

13. In place of true contrition, you taught me to be apologetic. I apologize continually. I apologize for my own existence, a fact that I cannot change. For years you told me I'd be sorry someday. I am.

14. You taught me to trust my own incompetence and even now won't let me mash potatoes without your direct supervision. "Don't run the mixer so fast that you get them all over," you say, as if in my home, the walls are covered with big white lumps. I can't mow a lawn or hang tinsel on a Christmas tree or paint a flat surface in your presence without you watching, worried, pointing out the unevenness.

15. You taught me an indecent fear of sexuality. I'm not sure I have any left underneath this baked-on crust of shame and disgust. For years I worried because my penis hangs slightly to the left, and finally read in a book that this is within the realm of the normal, but then wondered, *What sort of person would read books like that?*

16. You have provided me with poor male role models, including the Sons of Knute, the Boosters Club, and others whose petulance, inertia, and ineptitude are legendary. I was taught to respect them: men who clung to tiny grudges for decades and were devoted to vanity, horse feathers, small potatoes—not travel but the rites of trunk loading and map reading and gas mileage; not faith but the building committee; not love but supper.

17. Listening to them, I was taught to keep quiet. Stupidity had the floor, always. Argument was impolite.

18. You instilled in me a paralyzing nostalgia for a time before I was born, a time when men were men and women were saintly, when children were obedient, industrious, asked no luxuries, entertained themselves, and knew right from wrong. *I*, on the other hand, was a symptom of everything going to hell in a handbasket. I was *left* to wonder why I bothered to be born.

19. You brought me up to respect fastidiousness as incarnate virtue, Christianity made evident. As a tiny child, I lined up my string beans in a row on the plate, taking exactly three per bite. I hesitated to eat the mashed potatoes, lest the little gravy lake spill. I kept useless collections of stamps, seashells, postcards, rocks, delighting in their deadly neatness. In our home, all surfaces were meant to be bare; emptiness was the ideal. The fear of dust (amathophobia) was endemic. One little book lying on the floor: "The house is a mess. Why can't you ever put things back when you're done with them?" We were passionate about snow shoveling and made nice, even banks. In summer I edged the lawn, trimmed around trees, attacked dandelions. When Grandpa died, we tended his grave zealously, kneeling at the stone to landscape his resting place. "He was a good man," someone said once in the cemetery. "Ja," you said. "I've been thinking of applying a little Turf Builder. And maybe a fungicide."

20. In our theology, hard work was its own justification, a guard against corruption. Thus, we never bought an automatic dishwasher or a self-cleaning oven or a self-propelled mower with bag attachment, believing they would lead to degeneracy. We raked the grass clippings into a pile and later burned them. We did not use them for garden mulch because mulching kept weeds down and it was important that children weed the garden, slaving through the long, hot afternoons. It was good for them. It kept them from moral turpitude.

21. Suffering was its own reward, to be preferred to pleasure. As Lutherans, we viewed pleasure with suspicion. Birth control was never an issue with us. Nor was renunciation of pleasures of the flesh. We never enjoyed them in the first place. We were born to suffer. Pain was pooh-poohed. If you broke your leg, you walked home and applied ice. Don't complain. Don't baby yourself. Our mothers ironed sheets, underwear, even

in July. Our fathers wore out their backs at heavy, senseless labor, pulled their own teeth, lived with massive hemorrhoids. When Grandpa had his heart attack, he took one aspirin and went to bed early. We children suffered through dull, repetitive schoolwork, under the lash of sadistic teachers. Punishment was good for you, deserved or not; if you hadn't done wrong, well, then it was for last time.

22. A year ago, a friend offered to give me a back rub. I declined vociferously. You did this to me.

23. Two years ago I carried a box-spring mattress up four flights of stairs, declining offers of help, and did something to my back that still hurts. I didn't see a doctor but did buy a different mattress (orthopedic). Someone helped me carry it up and I felt guilty and kept saying, "No. Really. I got it now," all the way up as my back killed me and my eyes filled with tears.

24. Recently I dropped my air conditioner on my foot. I think this is related.

25. Despite the bum foot, I kept running four miles per day. I love the misery of running. I love the misery of feeling I should run more, hundreds of miles, and do it on my knees.

26. You taught me to believe in quietness as a sign of good character, that a child who sat silently with hands folded was a child who had overcome temptation. In fact, I was only scared, but being a nice, quiet boy, I was offered as an example to other children, many of whom despise me to this day. I did not have to be shushed on Sunday afternoon but went about my glum business of cutting out pictures from the rotogravure and pasting them into a scrapbook, being careful not to snip too loud. I learned that quietness could be used to personify not only goodness, but also intelligence and sensitivity, and so I silently earned a small reputation as a boy of superior intellect, a little scholar, a little sunbeam in this dark world, while in fact I was smug and lethargic and dull as a mud turtle.

27. Even now, I go to someone's house and think I am being a good guest if I am very quiet, don't ask for anything, and refuse anything that's offered. This behavior makes other people think of me as a nincompoop.

28. I find it very hard to whoop it up, hail a pal, split a gut, cut a rug, have a ball, or make a joyful noise. I'm your boy, all right.

29. You taught me not to go overboard, lose my head, or make a big deal out of it, but to keep a happy medium, that the truth is in the middle. No extremes. Don't exaggerate. Hold your horses. Keep a lid on it. Save it for later. Be careful. Weigh the alternatives. Wear navy blue. Years later, I am constantly adjusting my feelings downward to achieve that fine balance of caution and melancholy.

30. You taught me not to be "unusual" for fear of what the neighbors would say. They were omniscient, able to see through walls. We knew they'd talk, because we always talked about them. We thought they were nuts, but still we shouldn't offend them.

31. Your theology wasn't happy about the idea of mercy and forgiveness, which only gave comfort to enemies, and so, although you recited the Lord's Prayer every Sunday, you remembered your debtors and managed not to speak to certain people—a major feat when you live in a town so small and attend the same church as they, an act of true dedication. In your behalf, I still dislike Bunsens. I have no idea why.

32. Your own mistakes you managed to explain to your own satisfaction. When you hurt people, you explained that you didn't mean to. When you gossiped malicious gossip, you explained that "everyone knows this—and besides, it's true." You had a good reason for every dumb thing you did, which you said I would understand someday. I don't. I don't understand it at all.

33. *"Oh, I think you can do without that."* Your words come back to me when I look at a new sport coat. Good Scottish tweed, it costs $130, and when I try it on, it makes me feel smart and lucky and substantial, but you're right, I can do without it, and so I will. *"You can get a perfectly good one at Sears for half the price."* If I bought the $130 one, pride would leak in and rot my heart. Who do I think I am?

34. For fear of what it might do to me, you never paid a compliment, and when other people did, you beat it away from me with a stick. "He certainly is looking nice and grown up." *He'd look a lot nicer if he did something about his skin.* "That's wonderful that he got that job." *Yeah, well, we'll see how long it lasts.* You trained me so well, I now perform this service for myself. I deflect every kind word directed to me, and my denials are much more extravagant than the praise. "Good speech." *Oh, it was way too long, I didn't know what I was talking about, I was just blathering on and on, I was glad when it was*

*over.* I do this under the impression that it is humility—a becoming quality in a person. Actually, I am starved for a good word, but after the long drought of my youth, no word is quite good enough. "Good" isn't enough. Under this thin veneer of modesty lies a monster of greed. I drive away faint praise, beating my little chest, waiting to be named Sun-God, King of America, Idol of Millions, Bringer of Fire, the Great Haji, Thundar the Boy Giant. I don't want to say, "Thanks, glad you liked it." I want to say, "Rise, my people. Remove your faces from the carpet, stand, look me in the face."

35. The fear of poverty haunts me. You weren't poor, but you anticipated the possibility by believing you were.

36. The fear of illness. You were seldom ill, but you were always prepared to be.

37. Your illnesses were the result of exhaustion by good works, mine the result of having disobeyed you and not worn a scarf, not taken my vitamins. I crawl into bed like a dog and feel not only unwell but unworthy. If someone came in to shoot me, I'd turn on the light so he could take better aim.

38. The fear of poverty and illness, brought on by a sudden craving for cheap wine. A flaw in my character, a weak seam, and one day I bend down to tie my shoes and hear a rip in my head, and on the way to work I pick up a gallon of muscatel and spend my lunch hour in the alley. A month later, I have no job, no house, no car, and my nose is dark purple and swollen to the size of an eggplant. My voice is like sandpaper, I cough up gobs of phlegm, my liver feels like a sandbag. My teeth are rotten stumps. I crap in my pants and lurch toward strangers, mumbling about spare change. The flaw was created by disobeying you. "Someday you'll find out," you said, and I probably will.

39. Damn.

40. Damn.

41. Damn.

42. Damn.

[Three pages missing.]

56. In our house, work was a weapon, used as punishment, also to inspire guilt. You waited until I sat in a chair and read the funnies, then you charged in: "How can you *sit* with this mess all around you?" I looked

down. One lonely sock on the floor, a Juicy Fruit wrapper on the table. You snatched them up, sighed as if your heart was broken, and stalked out. A great sigh, so loud it could be heard in the back of the balcony. You worked your fingers to the bone, and did anyone lift a finger to help? No, they didn't. When I lifted a finger, you told me it was the wrong finger and I was lifting it the wrong way. When I vacuumed, suddenly vacuuming became an exact science, a branch of physics, and I was doing it all wrong—you snatched the hose away and said, "Here, I might as well do it myself," which was what you intended all along.

57. You taught me that, no matter what I thought, it was probably wrong. The world is fundamentally deceptive. The better something looks, the more rotten it probably is down deep. Some people were fooled but not you. You could always see the underlying truth, and the truth was ugly. Roosevelt was a drunk and that was that. New Deal? What New Deal? A sham, from beginning to end. There was no Depression; a person could get work if they really tried. There was more to everything than anyone knew. This teaching has led me, against my better judgment, to suspect people of trying to put one over. At the checkout counter, I lean forward to catch the girl if she tries to finesse an extra ten cents on the peaches. That's how Higgledy-Piggledy makes a profit. That's why cashiers ring up the goods so fast—to confuse us.

58. Believing there is always more than meets the eye defeats the sense of sight. Always looking for hidden meanings, a person misses the lovely surface of the world, even in spring. Surely those green leaves are hiding bare branches. If you look hard enough, you will glimpse them: dark, malevolent, and a big trunk that, if you ran into it hard enough, would kill you.

59. Nonetheless, you set store by a certain orderly look to things. Dinner was at noon, supper at five thirty. This is so ingrained in me that I eat whether I'm hungry or not. I eat everything put before me. It is a sign that I am good.

60. Clean clothes made us respectable.

61. A clean house distinguished us from colored people.

62. Bigotry is never a pleasant subject so you didn't bring it up but you stuck by your guns anyway. Indians were drunks, Jews were thieves, and the colored were shiftless. Where you got this, I don't know, because there

were none of them around, but you believed it more absolutely for the utter lack of evidence. *Everyone* knew about those people. It was common sense.

63.—67. [Obliterated by beverage stain.]

68. Everything was set in place in your universe, and you knew what everything and everybody was, whether you had ever seen them or not. You could glance at strangers and size them up instantly. An article of clothing, a phrase from their lips, a look in their eye—you knew who they were, and you were seldom generous in your assessments. "She certainly thinks a lot of *herself.*" "I'll bet that's not *his* wife." "If that man's not a crook, then today's not Sunday," you said one Sunday. It was something about the shape of his head. You could tell. They couldn't fool you. And now I do this myself. I adopted the mirror reverse of your prejudices and I apply them viciously. I detest neat-looking people like myself and people who look industrious and respectable. I sneer at them as middleclass. In elections, I vote automatically against Scandinavian names.

69. In fact, you imbued me with the sensitivity of a goat. I say vicious things about old friends to people I barely know. I say vicious things to people's faces and then explain that I was kidding. I am truly cavalier toward the suffering of innocent people, including that which I myself cause. The other day, I almost ran down an old man in a crosswalk. I hadn't seen him. My friend grabbed my arm and yelled, and I slammed on the brakes. Rather than apologize to the man, I turned and explained to my friend that I hadn't seen him. And I hadn't. I didn't even see him after I stopped and he stood there, dazed and terrified. I don't really see anybody.

70. When I hear about deprivation and injustice in the world, I get up and change the channel.

71. What can I do? It's not my fault. I didn't make them. God did. It's his world—let him take care of it.

72. Anyway, I was brought up to believe that whatever happens to people is their own fault. There were few if any disasters that you couldn't explain by citing the mistakes made by the victims. "She never should have married him." "He never should have been there in the first place." Even if you had to go back thirty years, you could find where they took the wrong fork in the road that led directly to their house burning down, their car being hit by a truck, their hands being eaten by corn pickers.

73. If they had been more like you, they would have been all right. But they weren't paying attention. They lacked your strong sense of the cruelty and hopelessness of the world.

74. You misdirected me as surely as if you had said the world is flat and north is west and two plus two is four; that is, not utterly wrong, just wrong enough so that when I took the opposite position—the world is mountainous, north is east—I was wrong, too, and your being wrong about the world and north made me spend years trying to come up with the correct sum of two and two, other than four. *You gave me the wrong things to rebel against.* My little boat sailed bravely against the wind, straight into the rocks. Your mindless monogamy made me vacillate in love, your compulsive industry made me a prisoner of sloth, your tidiness made me sloppy, your materialism made me wasteful.

75. I wasted years in diametrical opposition, thinking you were completely mistaken, and wound up living a life *based more on yours* than if I'd stayed home.

76. Because you always went to bed at ten, I stayed up half the night chain smoking (you were opposed to cigarettes) and drinking straight gin (you didn't drink), and, given time, might have cut off my arm, it being yet another thing you never would have done.

77. I wasted some good years thinking proudly that I wasn't anything like you. Having grown up with ugly wallpaper, I painted all my walls off-white and thought I'd finally arrived. Bought a white couch, yours having been purple. My place looks like February.

78. I resist washing.

79. I revolted by becoming a sensitive person, which I am not. I hate folk music. I don't care for most of the sensitive people I feel obligated to hang out with. Many of them play guitars and write songs about their feelings. I have to pack up my Percy Faith records when they come and put the box in the bedroom closet and pile winter coats on it, and despite the mothballs I'm afraid they'll take one sniff and say, "You like light classical, don't you?" I pour a round of Löwenbräu, being careful not to pour along the side but straight down so the beer can express itself, and they say, "Did you ever try Dockendorf?" It's made by the Dockendorf family from hand-pumped water in their ancient original family brewery in an unspoiled Pennsylvania village where the barley is hauled in by Amish

families who use wagons with oak beds. Those oak beds give Docken-dorf its famous flavor. These beer bores, plus the renovators of Victorian houses, the singer-songwriters, the runners, the connoisseurs of northern Bengali cuisine, the collectors of everything Louis Armstrong recorded between August 1925 and June 1928, his seminal period—they are driving me inexorably toward life as a fat man in a bungalow swooning over sweet-and-sour pork. You drove me toward *them*.

80. This is one I can't say. It's true and it's important, having to do with sexual identity, but if I said it, I'd hear you saying, "How can you *say* that?" and I know I'd feel guilty. So I won't. *You* know what I mean.

81. Another thing of the same sort.

82. Another.

83. Guilt. Guilt as a child, then anger at you for filling me with guilt, then guilt at the anger. Then I tried to relieve *that* guilt by presenting you with a wonderful trip to Los Angeles to see your aunt. You protested that I didn't need to, then you went, and you conspired to make it awful. You cashed in the first-class plane tickets and flew tourist, you canceled the reservation at the Beverly Wilshire and stayed at a cheap motel in Torrance by the freeway, then you came home miserable (but happy) and gave me a refund.

84. I took you to a famous steakhouse on your anniversary. You agonized over the menu and ordered the cheapest thing. I pleaded, I argued. I ordered the prime rib. I felt guilty as I ate it, just as you intended.

85. With the refund from the trip, I bought you a pearl necklace and a pair of gold earrings. You never wore them. "I'm afraid of losing them," you said. "Here? In the house?" I said. "You never can tell," you said.

86. All those birthdays and Christmases, when you turned to me and said, "You shouldn't have," you really meant it. You were the author of the story, not me, and it was supposed to be about generous parents and an ingrate son. Once or twice, dark marital suffering was hinted at, with the clear intimation that you had stuck together for my sake. I felt wretched for months.

87. A scene, repeated thousands of times:
YOU (*in the easy chair*): Dear? As long as you're up, would you mind—
ME (*in the doorway*): What?

YOU (*rising*): Oh, never mind. I'll do it myself.

ME: *What?* I'll do it.

YOU (*sighing*): No, that's all right. You'd never find it. (Or "You might burn yourself." Or "I'd just have to do it myself anyway." Or "It's nothing.")

88. A scene from early childhood: Our Sunday school class learned "Joy to the World" for the Christmas program. You asked me to sing it for the aunts and uncles when they came to dinner. I said no. You said yes. I said no. You said, "Someday when I'm dead and in my coffin, maybe you'll look down and remember the times I asked you to do things and you wouldn't." So I sang, terrified of them and terrified about your death. You stopped me halfway through. You said, "Now, come on. You can sing it better than that."

89. A few years later, when I sang the part of Curly in *Oklahoma!* and everybody else said it was wonderful, you said, "I told him for years he could sing and he wouldn't listen to me."

90. I did listen to you—that's most of my problem. Everything you said went in one ear and right down my spine. Such as, "You're never going to make anything of yourself." When I was laid off from a job, you couldn't believe it wasn't for something I had done, something so awful that I wouldn't tell you.

91. Everything I said had hidden meaning for you, even "I'm going to bed." "You can't even spend a *few minutes* talking to your parents?" you said.

92. Every tiny disagreement was an ultimate blow to you. "Is this the thanks we get after all we've done?"

93. My every act was a subject of study: "What are you doing?" you asked a million times. "Why didn't you do it before?" (Or "Can't it wait until later?") "Why do it *here*?" "Why are you so quiet?" "I'm thinking." "About what?"

94. My posture, facial expression (if any), tone of voice, gait—all were of constant critical interest as you strove to achieve a perfect balance in me. "Sit up. Don't slouch." Then, "Relax. You make me nervous just to look at you." "Why such a gloomy look?" Then, "Wipe that smirk off your face." "Pick up your feet." Then, "Can't you walk without sounding like a herd of elephants?" "Speak up. Don't mumble." "Keep your voice down."

95. Now you call me on the phone to ask, "Why don't you ever call us? Why do you shut us out of your life?" So I start to tell you about my life, but you don't want to hear it. You want to know why I didn't call. I didn't call because I don't need to talk to you anymore. Your voice is in my head, talking constantly from morning till night. I keep the radio on, but I still hear you and will hear you until I die, when I will hear you say, "I told you," and then something else will happen.

# 28

# Lutheran Song

I was raised in Iowa, went to Concordia,
Swedish, I'm proud to say.
Got a job at Lutheran Brotherhood,
And I never was sick one day.
Bought a house in south Minneapolis
Over by Cedar Lake.
If you ask me, this latest merger
Was nothing but a big mistake.
Now I have nothing against Episcopalians;
I believe in an open door.
I'm sure it's good to get new ideas,
But we never did it that way before.

Praise heaven, I believe.
Praise heaven, I believe.
I'm a Lutheran, a Lutheran—it is my belief;
I am a Lutheran guy.
We may have merged with another church,
But I'm a Lutheran till I die.

We are a modest people
And we never make a fuss,
And it sure would be a better world
If they were all as modest as us.
We do not go for whooping it up

Or a lot of yikkety-yak.
When we say hello, we avert our eyes,
And we always sit in the back.
We sit in the pew where we always sit,
And we do not shout "Amen!"
And if anyone yells or waves their hands,
They're not invited back again.

I'm a Lutheran, a Lutheran—it is my belief;
I am a Lutheran guy.
We may have merged with another church,
But I'm a Lutheran till I die.

We've got chow mein noodles on tuna hotdish
And Jell-O with cottage cheese
And chocolate bars and banana cream pie—
No wonder we're on our knees.
This is the church where we sing "Amen"
At the end of every song.
The coffeepot is always on
'Cause the meetings are three hours long.
The blessed tie that binds our hearts
Is cream of mushroom soup.
We do not walk through the door alone;
We wait and go as a group.

Praise heaven, I believe.
Praise heaven, I believe.
I'm a Lutheran, a Lutheran—it is my belief;
I am a Lutheran guy.
We may have merged with another church,
But I'm a Lutheran till I die.

Episcopalians are proud of their faith;
You ought to hear 'em talk.
Who they got? They got Henry VIII

*Life among the Lutherans*

And we got J. S. Bach.
Henry VIII, he had six wives
Trying to make a son.
J. S. Bach had twenty-three children,
And wives, he had just one.
Henry VIII would marry a woman
And then her head would drop.
J. S. Bach had all those kids
'Cause his organ had no stop.

Praise heaven, I believe.
Praise heaven, I believe.
I'm a Lutheran, a Lutheran—it is my belief;
I am a Lutheran guy.
Episcopalians I don't mind,
But I'm a Lutheran till I die.

Once in a while we go to shows,
But a Lutheran is not a fan.
We don't whistle and we don't laugh;
We smile as loud as we can.
If you come to church, don't expect to be hugged;
Don't expect your hand to be shook.
If we need to know who you are,
We can look in the visitors' book.
I was raised to keep a lid on it,
Guard what you say or do.
A mighty fortress is our God,
So he must be Lutheran too.

Praise heaven, I believe.
Praise heaven, I believe.
I'm a Lutheran, a Lutheran—it is my belief;
I am a Lutheran guy.
Episcopalians I don't mind,
But I'm a Lutheran till I die.